Joanna Thompson

Vote for Love

Planet Girl

Dark Things

Weird opening question: do you believe in ghosts? I used to, **sort of.** I had my own private scary demons – I called them the "Dark Things". Yes, that's right, the Dark Things. I hated them.

The Dark Things were *sort of* ghosts, though they weren't white like your standard Caspar-type **ghoul**, of course – they were black. And they didn't rattle chains or drink blood. No, what they did was *much* worse: they jumped out at you if you went to the toilet at night, **grabbing for** your **ankles**. Needing the toilet after dark was, as you might imagine, a major trauma for me when I was a kid.

I grew up, of course, and found other Dark Things to worry about: boys! Ha! To be **honest**, I hadn't thought about the original Dark Things in years. Until now that is, as I lie here at 3 am, needing the toilet, in The Grange, my grandmother's house. I can't stop thinking about them now, unfortunately.

The reason is clear: my grandmother, Beatrice Milling-

+++ weird – eigenartig +++ sort of – irgendwie +++ ghoul – Ungeheuer +++ to grab for s.th. – nach etw. greifen +++ ankle – Knöchel +++ honest – ehrlich +++

ton, known to her loving but sometimes sarcastic family as the Queen Mother, died in her sleep last Tuesday – at almost exactly this time! – aged 83.

It was a peaceful death, they say. There's absolutely no reason why my grandmother should come back to **haunt** her loving but sarcastic family. She lived a good life and it's clear that she'll have taken the royal express train to heaven. She'll be drinking sherry and playing **bridge** with the Queen Mum and Queen Victoria there as we speak.

Even with that beautiful image firmly in my mind, I still can't *quite* convince myself to go to the toilet. It's right at the end of the hall and to get there, I'd have to walk past the room where my grandmother died. It's too **creepy**, **way** too creepy. The Dark Things will definitely **have it staked out**.

I'm crazy, *natürlich*. If something dark *did* grab me and I screamed, then a whole army of Bright Things would come running to help me: my mum and dad, my little brother Max and my Auntie Nora are all sleeping in various parts of the house. Even my Onkel Dieter from Eisenhüttenstadt is here, though he's certainly not bright.

And there's Sam, of course. Sam would definitely come running. In fact … that's not a bad idea. Well, it *is* an emergency. I need a big strong escort to the toilet now, it's clear. He's just the man for the job.

It's **insane**, of course, but I am totally, **utterly** desperate. I will wet the bed in a moment, otherwise, and that's

+++ to haunt s.b. – jmdn. heimsuchen +++ bridge – Kartenspiel +++ creepy – gruselig +++ way – *hier:* viel +++ to have s.th. staked out – etw. überwachen lassen +++ insane – verrückt +++ utterly – völlig +++

not a really cool look when you're 15, now is it? So I grab my phone, call Sam's mobile number, praying that he's left it switched on. He has! Hurrah! It rings and rings before finally a *very* sleepy-sounding voice says, "Emily?? What on earth …?"

"Can you come down?" I **hiss**. "It's really, really urgent!" Sam groans. "What … oh, **never mind**. You **nutter**. Yes, I'll come down." And my hero hangs up.

Sam, you might remember, is my boyfriend, my long-distance lover from Scotland. Right now, luckily, he's my very short-distance lover. Sam arrived here in Surrey yesterday and he's now about two metres away, **as the crow flies**, in the guest bedroom directly above me. My mother put him on a separate floor, partly to **preserve** my honour no doubt, but also because the only free bedroom on this floor would have been my grandmother's. And no one much liked the idea of Sam sleeping there, least of all Sam.

I can hear footsteps in the hall, soft, Sammy ones: it's the sound of **salvation**! Sam taps at the door … I'm saved! I **leap** out of bed and there he is. My hero! My hero who hasn't even **bothered** to put his glasses on: he's **squinting** at me. His hair is a mess, he looks totally exhausted. "This had better be good …" he mumbles, rubbing his eyes.

I'm embarrassed, of course, but sometimes a girl's got to do what a girl's got to do. "I need to *go*," I **mutter**,

+++ to hiss – zischen +++ never mind – schon gut +++ nutter – Spinner/in +++ as the crow flies – Luftlinie +++ to preserve – erhalten +++ salvation – Erlösung +++ to leap – springen +++ to bother – sich die Mühe machen +++ to squint – blinzeln +++ to mutter – murmeln

pulling him by the arm. "And I was too scared to *go* by myself …"

Sam looks at me in horror. "You got me out of bed at *three in the morning* to walk you to the bathroom??????"

It sounds so **selfish** when you put it like that! "Well, I needed to talk to you, too," I mumble, a bit weakly. Sam's mumbling something, too: bad, bad words. The Queen Mother would die if she heard that … oh, never mind.

Sam thinks about punching me in the face, decides it would take too much energy and finally bursts out laughing. "Oh, **for goodness sake**, move it!"

When Sam and me get back to my room, we have a little bit of a kiss. Partly to celebrate surviving The Spooky Toi-

+++ selfish – egoistisch +++ for goodness sake – um Himmels willen

let Trip and partly because Sam's earned one. It actually feels quite **naughty**, kissing Sam in my bedroom at this time in the morning. My mum would **freak**, probably, but I have to tell you – knowing that somehow makes the kissing feel even nicer.

Then it's time to talk. There's a lot to discuss. I've **barely** had a minute alone with Sam since my family and me found him standing on the doorstep of my grandmother's house when we arrived back from the **funeral**. Amazing. Sam had **trekked** about 600 kilometres and has run the risk of losing his part-time job – "they probably won't fire me!" he laughs – to be here with me now. Be honest, how many of all your 6.5 million Facebook "friends" or Twitter contacts would do that? Go on, count them. It's no more than two or three, I bet you. *Maximum.*

So, personally, I was **delighted** to see Sam. I have the strange feeling, however, that the rest of my family don't share in my joy. My parents, **for instance**, gave Sam more or less the same look that they used to give the half-dead birds our cat "Mr T" loved to **drag** into our flat in Berlin. I don't really understand why: my parents have never even met Sam before! They know I went to visit him in Scotland but I didn't talk about that trip much to them. So they can't be giving him the cold shoulder because they know how complicated our whole relationship has been, for instance.

+++ naughty – unartig +++ to freak – ausflippen +++ barely – kaum +++ funeral – Beerdigung +++ to trek – *hier:* reisen +++ delighted – erfreut +++ for instance – zum Beispiel +++ to drag – schleppen +++

Oh, come on, it has been! I'm not being dramatic, honestly. Sam and me seem to have been through a lot, even though we've only been going out for eleven months or so. Even the way we got together was stressful. Ah, sweet memories …

I thought all my Christmases had come at once when I met a charming boy named Ed Stanton, right after I arrived at Chalk Farm School for Girls in London last year. But Ed was no Santa: he grew bored with me after about eight minutes, it seemed, and was kind enough to **dump** me and then blog about it. The only good thing about the whole Ed Affair was that I made two great friends, Maudie and Kim, and … I met Sam – he played drums with Ed in their band, the Kitty Gagarins. Sam ended up helping me to get revenge on Ed and we started dating just after that. We had to be really careful at first, hiding our love away so that Ed wouldn't find out and **smash** Sam's head through his **tom toms**. And, frankly, if *that's* not a complicated start to a relationship, I don't know what is.

I thought Christmas for our relationship had actually come at, well, *Christmas*. But instead of kissing and drinking *Glühwein* from a shared cup, as we should have been, Sam and me faced our next crisis, a present from my **boggle-eyed** roommate Amanda Dobson. She flirted like crazy with Sam at the Christmas party. Sam, luckily, wasn't interested in her. Things between us should have settled down then, right? Am I right?

+++ to dump s.b. – mit jmdm. Schluss machen +++ to smash – zertrümmern +++ tom tom – Trommel +++ boggle-eyed – mit Glotzaugen +++

No such luck. Our next love challenge was waiting to jump out at us, like a Dark Thing: Sam's dad lost his job and got ill which meant Sam couldn't afford to stay in London any more. But Sam and me decided, being young and naïve, that we could make our relationship work, even with us both at opposite ends of the country. I would stay on in London and we would travel to see each other. True love, after all, has no **boundaries**.

Anyway, **to cut a long story short**, it seemed that true love wasn't stupid. True love did know *exactly* where its boundaries were. It was almost impossible to find the time to meet up. Once he got back to Scotland, Sam just seemed so busy with his family, the new band he'd found and his part-time job. I suppose I felt that he didn't need me any more …

… which might explain why I allowed myself to be interested in someone else – *Sportsfreund* Sebastian Junger, a boy from my old school in Berlin. I was wrong as it turned out – again, it's a long story – but the damage was done, somehow. Sam wasn't, like, *totally* enthusiastic about me having had Sebastian to visit me in London.

It's hard to believe that even after all that, Sam would still make the effort to come here to see me, isn't it? I **gaze at** him; he's **yawning** now. Then he falls back onto my bed and lies there for a moment, **blinking** like an **owl**. "Come over here," he says, sleepily. "Tell me what's on your mind, toilet girl."

+++ boundary – Grenze +++ to cut a long story short – um es kurz zu machen +++ to gaze at s.b./s.th. – jmdn./etw. anschauen +++ to yawn – gähnen +++ to blink – blinzeln +++ owl – Eule +++

What's on Toilet Girl's Mind

What's on my mind? What's *not* on my mind, more like. It's 4 am and I lie in Sam's arms – sorry, Mum – and give it to him: the list of some of the things that are really, really bothering me, right now.

First and worst, my grandmother has just died, obviously. It's not just that I miss her, I also have a seriously **guilty conscience**. Grandma was so kind to me and how did I repay her? By laughing at her a lot, it seems now. And rolling my eyes and looking at my watch every time I had to talk to her on the phone. And by never visiting her. I'm a bad person. Very, very bad.

I can't even remember when the last conversation I had with my grandmother was. **Get** this – she had called me at school and left a message saying there was *something important* she had to tell me and *I never called her back.* Incredible. Lock me up and throw away the key.

I didn't take her very seriously, of course. My grandmother loved to talk. She permanently had Something Important She Wanted to Tell Me. It was usually "urgent" things like my hockey socks needing replacing.

+++ guilty conscience – schlechtes Gewissen +++ to get – *hier:* verstehen +++

But now, I can't stop wondering – what was it that she wanted to tell me? What if it really had been a matter of life and death? What if Grandma had already known that she was dying? What if she wanted my help? That thought kills me, **incidentally**, *it kills me.*

I've been worrying about this non-stop. In the days after Grandma died, I **kept praying** that we would find a letter addressed to me, Emily Hausmann, her only granddaughter. I could imagine it so clearly. My mother would hand the letter to me, and I would **tear** it open and read it, hearing Grandma's voice in my head, just like you do in films:

Dear Emily,
By the time you read this letter, I shall be gone. My death was totally peaceful and I didn't suffer. I don't ***blame*** *you* ***for*** *never calling me or coming to see me before I died. You're young. You were busy having fun. I'm cool with that.* ***By the way****, the totally important thing that I had to tell you was that Broughton's, the uniform shop, is having a sale in October and hockey skirts are reduced by 20%! If you bought two now, that would mean that you would have a* ***spare*** *one for next season! Goodbye my dear. I must go now – the real Queen Mum wants to have a chat and eat* ***shepherd's pie****. I love you and all the best.*

+++ incidentally – im Übrigen +++ to keep doing s.th. – etw. immer weiter tun +++ to pray – beten +++ to tear – reißen +++ to blame s.b. for s.th. – jmdm. die Schuld an etw. geben +++ by the way – übrigens +++ spare – extra +++ shepherd's pie – Auflauf aus Hackfleisch und Kartoffelbrei +++

Everything would be explained. I could sleep easy again. But no such letter has **turned up**, frustratingly.

I tell Sam all of this and he sighs deeply, then **sneezes**. He's been scratching his nose a lot as I lie **bearing** my soul with my head on his chest. "Oh, I'm sorry! Everything is so … perfumed in this house, isn't it? I think I'm allergic to something here – **lavender**? **Patchouli**?"

Sam wipes his nose on a **hanky** taken from a pink, **frilly** box beside my bed. Then he says slowly, "You loved your grandma. She couldn't have known she was dying and she wouldn't have bothered you with that anyway. She would have gone to a doctor. It was probably nothing. And …" he **hesitates**, "it *is* hard to find the time to visit someone, even when you care about them a lot. We know all about that."

Yes, we do. But I don't want to have the "Where is our relationship going?" conversation with Sam just yet. I change the subject and move on quickly to the next **item** on my List of Things Bothering Me.

Here it is. I **mentioned** it before. Ever since Sam arrived, my family have been acting really strangely around him. Don't get me wrong, of course: they were behaving strangely long *before* he arrived. **Grief** does weird things to you. My father, for instance, doesn't know what to feel **at all**. He and my grandmother never really

+++ to turn up – auftauchen +++ to sneeze – nießen +++ to bear – stützen +++ lavender – Lavendel +++ patchouli – Patschuli +++ hanky – Papiertaschentuch +++ frilly – auffällig +++ to hesitate – zögern +++ item – Gegenstand +++ to mention – erwähnen +++ grief – Kummer +++ not ... at all – überhaupt nicht +++

liked each other and right now, I think Dad's guilty and relieved and sad and happy, all at the same time. It's like living with a walking, talking **mood chart**.

But since Sam arrived, everything here in Wonderland has got **curiouser** and curiouser. Even Auntie Nora has been strange with him. She disappeared after the funeral and only turned up here at The Grange again late yesterday evening. Sam and me were still sitting in the kitchen when she arrived and Nora's first words when she saw him weren't, for instance, *How nice!* or *What a surprise!* but something like: *Did the* ***lawyers*** *write to you about the* ***will****?*

I have no idea what Nora was talking about and she won't tell me. My parents are also keeping *stumm.* Mum keeps saying they'll *explain everything* soon. She's been polite to Sam but she just seems **suspicious** of him, too. She's asked him about 47 million billion times why he came here. *Just to see Emily?????* Like it was *impossible* that anyone would want to come all this way to visit me. Cheers, Ma! So, what I want to know is – what's going on? What are they all so nervous about?

Sam **shrugs his shoulders**, which is a strange feeling when you're lying on one of them, I have to say. He says calmly, "Yes, well, your grandmother must have left me something in her will. I suppose me coming here makes it look like I'm here for the cash."

+++ mood chart – Stimmungsbarometer +++ curious – seltsam +++ lawyer – Anwalt/Anwältin +++ will – Testament +++ suspicious – misstrauisch +++ to shrug one's shoulders – mit den Schultern zucken +++

That must be it, of course. I like Sam for being so direct. He just comes out and says what we both suspect: *I'm in your Grandma's will.*

It wouldn't be a total surprise. The Queen Mother had offered Sam money before. I had **begged** her to pay for him to stay on at St Dougan's boys' school after he told me he would have to leave London. Sam was **insulted** and **furious** with me – it caused yet another storm in our relationship. Oops, forgot to tell you about that one before.

"What do you think she left you?" I mutter.

Sam says softly, "I'm hoping it's her granddaughter." We laugh but it's clear – he can hardly keep his eyes open. I really don't want him to fall asleep here (try explaining that one to my parents!) so I send him back up to his own room. There are other things I'd love to talk to him about but they'll have to wait.

The following morning, I oversleep – if you can call sleeping from 4.30 am until 9.30 am "oversleeping". I'm the last one down to breakfast and everyone is finishing up as I arrive. Even poor Sam, who couldn't have slept any longer than me, has obviously been up for a while. I'm starving and I spot some cold-looking toast standing in a **rack** shaped like a **poodle**. I grab a piece and take a seat next to Onkel Dieter. Sam's talking about football in a gentle voice with Max. He winks at me. Sam, not Max.

I butter my toast, angrily. I'm **cross** with myself for not waking up sooner. Sam has to leave this evening to get the

+++ to beg – bitten +++ insulted – beleidigt +++ furious – wütend +++ rack – Toastständer +++ poodle – Pudel +++ cross – sauer +++

overnight bus back to Glasgow and I still need to discuss so many things with him.

But so do some other people in the room, it seems. I reach for the marmalade and catch my mother's eye. *Oh, right, the will.* Mum says curtly, "Sam and Emily, it's time to discuss … **legal** matters."

It's almost like they've **rehearsed** it. As soon as my mother says the word "will", everyone else in the room – except Dad – gets to their feet and leaves. Auntie Nora is leading Max by the hand and trying to smile politely, as Onkel Dieter says to her, "Now zay talk money, *oder*? Bizness."

+++ legal – rechtlich +++ to rehearse – proben +++

My mother waits until the three of them have left the room, then shuts the door quietly. I'm just trying to get my toast down as fast as I can before we talk "bizness". I can't bear to look at Sam.

Mum then slowly **produces** an envelope from a **dresser** near the table and says, "Sam, I understand my mother had offered to help you with your schooling before?"

Sam **blushes**. Well, of course he does. This is embarrassing. We were right, of course. The Queen Mother has left Sam money. I just hope he doesn't react like he did last time and punch my mother in the face or something.

Mum obviously wants Dad to **break the news** "officially" because she looks at him, very hard. When that doesn't work, she **elbows** him. Dad finally says, "Oh, right. Well, there's some good news for the two of you. Beatrice, I mean, Emily's grandmother, has left you both very large sums of money. For your education, of course."

I **gasp**. I hadn't even thought about *me* being in the will, too! Honest. It's terrible, obviously, but somewhere deep inside me, a tiny, **greedy** voice whispers, *I am rich!!*

Maybe my mum spots the little pound signs in my eyes. Maybe she knows only too well what I would do with a large sum of money in Top Shop. Anyway, for whatever reason, she says very quickly, "I repeat, Emily, the money is in a **trust fund** for your *education*. Specifically your education at Chalk Farm School."

+++ to produce – hervorholen +++ dresser – Kommode +++ to blush – rot werden +++ to break the news – die Neuigkeiten verkünden +++ to elbow – mit dem Ellbogen anstoßen +++ to gasp – nach Luft schnappen +++ greedy – gierig +++ trust fund – Treuhandfond +++

She smiles a bit stiffly at Sam: "Or at St Dougan's, in your case." Sam nods. He's doing his best to smile back at my mother but he's really uncomfortable, I know it. He's drumming his fingers – that's a sure sign he's **tense**.

And then Dad does what Dad does best; he "drops the bomb" into the conversation. He **coughs**. Without taking his eyes off Sam, he says, "Mrs Millington's lawyers actually wanted to write a letter to you this week, telling you, Sam. It's a bit strange you turning up like this … you really didn't know about the money?"

I gasp again. Is Dad actually accusing Sam – Mr **Integrity**! – of knowing about the will, of coming here looking for money? Or of influencing my grandma, like he was some **weirdass** gigolo? Oh man. I could **strangle** my father. How **dare** he?

Sam takes it remarkably well. He was drumming his fingers a lot before, as he always does when he's nervous, but now he's stopped. He's not making them into a fist to punch my father, it seems. Instead, Sam says calmly, "No, I never met Mrs Millington. I never even spoke to her, actually."

Sam looks to me for confirmation and I nod. Sam really couldn't have known, could he? It's just not possible. It's not like he and the Queen Mother lived around the corner from each other.

I'm suddenly curious about what else is in the will. "She didn't leave all her money to us, did she?" I **blurt out**.

+++ tense – angespannt +++ to cough – husten +++ integrity – Anstand +++ weirdass – extrem eigenartig +++ to strangle – erwürgen +++ to dare – wagen +++ to blurt out – herausplatzen +++

Mum blushes. "No, most of it goes to ..." She hangs her head, almost **as though** she's ashamed. "Myself, Nora. Max, of course – there's also a trust fund set up for him. She left some money to her housekeeper. And she left rather a lot to Chalk Farm School itself."

No one speaks. Finally, Sam says very politely, "Could you give me a few minutes alone with Emily, Mr and Mrs Hausmann?"

Mum and Dad aren't **thrilled**, I can tell, but they do get to their feet and leave the kitchen. *Ten minutes*, says my mother firmly. As soon as they're gone, Sam whispers, "Man, Emily, I had no idea your grandmother was *that* rich! Where did she get all her money anyway?"

I'm furiously buttering another slice of toast – I'm still hungry. I suddenly realise I don't really know why the Queen Mother was so rich. My grandfather had owned a factory that sold knives. That's about all I can remember.

I look at Sam **blankly**. "Knives," I say slowly. "It had something to do with ... knives." I hold the knife I've just been buttering my toast with up in the air, as if Sam might not actually know what the word "knife" means.

And before I know it, Sam and me are **giggling** again. It's all *crazeeee*. I feel so sad still, so sad. It's exciting, too, having all this money suddenly, even if it can only be spent at the boring old Royal Bank of Learning.

Sam stops laughing suddenly. I realise he knows

+++ as though – als ob +++ thrilled – begeistert +++ blank – ausdruckslos +++ to giggle – kichern +++

exactly what he's going to do already. He doesn't need to discuss it with me. He just wants to tell me first.

He looks at me, my blue-eyed boy, completely sincere. "Your grandmother must have been an incredible woman. I wish I'd known her, I really do. She was totally **passionate** about education, wasn't she?"

It's true. It's funny – now that she's gone, I see the Queen Mother totally differently. I always thought she pushed me to go to Chalk Farm School as a matter of family **pride**. I never really thought that it might just be because she wanted me to go to a good school.

Sam **takes a deep breath**. Here it comes: his decision. I've got no idea what he's going to say, nor what I actually want to hear. There's part of me that would like to scream *TAKE THE MONEY!* at him, as though we were in some weird game show called *SHAPE YOUR LIFE!* or something. There's another bit of me that respects him for saying no last time and knows that money wasn't the only reason Sam went back to Scotland. He wanted to be near his family, to be able to help them out.

And, sure enough, Sam's made the decision I can respect. He says quietly, "It still wouldn't feel right to have someone else pay for my education. And, really, I don't want to come back to London. It took me a while to feel at home in Scotland again but I'm loving it now. I'm there for my family when they need me … you can't put a price on that."

+++ passionate – leidenschaftlich +++ pride – Stolz +++ to take a deep breath – tief Luft holen +++ to shape – formen, gestalten +++

Sam's looking at me nervously now. We both know that there should be one reason for Sam to at least *think* about accepting the Queen Mother's offer from **beyond** the **grave**: it would bring our relationship back from the dead. Sam coming back to London is our only chance, we both know that.

I don't say anything and Sam doesn't **either**. He doesn't make any promises to come down more often from Scotland in the future. He doesn't say, in a **determined** voice, as he always did before: *We'll find a way!* Because … we didn't find a way. Long-distance love – ha! Long-distance **torture**, more like. We've learned our lesson. It's time to move on. Where to, I've no idea.

We don't **break up** officially here. **Neither** of us says anything concrete. It's clear it's not the time. Even Ed Stanton wouldn't have tried to break up with me right after my grandmother had just died, probably. Possibly. But the decision to split up has been made, silently, automatically. Now all we can do is just to try and enjoy the couple of hours we have left.

+++ beyond – jenseits +++ grave – Grab +++ not ... either – auch nicht +++ determined – entschlossen +++ torture – Folter +++ to break up – Schluss machen, sich trennen +++ neither – keiner +++

The Flashback Scene

Sam gets to his feet. He **peers** out of the kitchen window. "Listen, I can see your parents from here. They're in the garden. I'll go and tell them what I've decided. Then I'll go upstairs and throw my **stuff** together. I'll have to leave in a couple of hours. Maybe we could walk to the train station. It would give us some time alone."

I nod. Sam leaves the room, off to shock my parents. I sit very still for a moment. It's over, I think. *It's over.* I have a strange feeling in my chest – my heart breaking? Well, not really, not yet. It's my stomach **rumbling.** I'm still starving.

I suddenly remember that, even in my grief, I **couldn't help but** notice my grandmother's housekeeper arriving this morning with a **wicked**-looking apple pie. My entire family would have been **wiped out** by starvation by now if it hadn't been for her. No one would have managed to cook anything, I'm sure. I'm not sure anyone still knows what a "shop" is.

I want that pie! I've just opened the fridge door and am

+++ to peer – spähen +++ stuff – Sachen, Zeug +++ to rumble – *hier:* knurren +++ can't help but – nichts dafür können +++ wicked – *hier:* super +++ to wipe out – ausradieren +++

leaning in for the **kill**, when the kitchen door opens again. It's Auntie Nora. She laughs – I'm holding the huge **dish** of pie in my hand and must look really guilty. "Sorry," she giggles. "I left some letters here." She nods towards a **pile** sitting on the kitchen **counter**. "Don't let me stop you!"

She moves to gather up the letters. I know what kind of letters they are, of course – letters of **condolence** we received for Grandma. Thousands of them. Nora is bravely trying to answer them all: the Queen Mother would have expected it.

Nora sighs. "I've no idea how I'm going to manage this ..." Then she smiles at me. She really did need the letters right now *probably* but I think she'd also like to know what just happened, too. She sits down next to me and watches me **carve** myself off a huge **chunk** of pie. "How did Sam react? Was he as angry as last time?"

"He was pretty cool about it," I mutter. "But he won't take the money." I start to stuff my face with pie. Sorry, but I'm emotionally **drained**. And that *burns* the calories!

Nora **beams at** me. She loves a bit of moral integrity. "Ah, Sam's a good boy. I'm not keeping my money either." Nora talks a bit about the school in Afghanistan, the **orphanage** in **Moldova**, all the places that she wants to give her **inheritance** to. Then she says, more sadly, "But I thought I might keep a little bit and buy a new car. Something a bit greener. That would have made Mother

+++ kill – Beute +++ dish – Teller +++ pile – Stapel +++ counter – Theke +++ condolence – Beileid +++ to carve – säbeln +++ chunk – Stück +++ drained – ausgelaugt +++ to beam at s.b. – jmdn. anstrahlen +++ orphanage – Waisenhaus +++ Moldova – Moldavien +++ inheritance – Erbe +++

happy." (The Queen Mother hated Nora's coolio **vintage** car.)

I'm still filling my face with the world's greatest pie as Nora talks. You wouldn't think I was **anxious**. But I am. The other thing that I've been really, really worrying about **concerns** Nora. This is the first time I've had her alone. It's my moment in time.

But before I try to find out, let me finish my pie! While I eat that, I'll give you a quick *Flashback Scene*. Gives you a chance to **catch up**, me a chance to fill up! Ha!

Flashback to My Grandmother's Funeral: Here's the

+++ vintage – altmodisch, retro +++ anxious – besorgt +++ to concern – betreffen +++ to catch up – aufholen +++

scene. The funeral service is over. My whole family are now standing in a sad **row**, lined up outside the church, shaking hands with everyone and thanking them for coming: it's what one does, **apparently**.

My hand's already quite **sore** when I realise that the next person to shake it will be *Miss Bardwell.* Who's Miss Bardwell? Oh come on, where have you been? Miss Bardwell – how to explain her role in my life? Put it this way: she is everything and nothing to me. She's my housemistress and Latin teacher back at school. She was at Chalk Farm School **back in the day** with Nora, whom she hated then and has hated even more, ever since our Christmas party, when Nora sort of kissed Mr Michaels, Miss Bardwell's **fiancé**. Mr Michaels then dumped Miss Bardwell. That had nothing to do with Nora, **though**, I swear.

Miss Bardwell is not here at the funeral today because she hates Nora or me, I tell myself **sternly**, as I watch her moving towards me. She's here because she was sort of friends with the Queen Mother. And it's true: Miss Bardwell really isn't interested in me. She barely says a word to me. I can't help but notice, however, that she's staring **intently** at Nora, who's at the end of the line.

Hmmm. They'll be fine, I think. I mean, it's a funeral. No one's going to pick a fight at a funeral! Still, I can hardly bear to watch as Nora holds her hand out to my

+++ row – Reihe +++ apparently – offensichtlich +++ to be sore – weh tun +++ back in the day – *hier:* in ihrer Jugend +++ fiancé/e – Verlobte/r +++ though – trotzdem +++ stern – ernst +++ intent – unverwandt +++

housemistress. And luckily, I *really* can't watch the **encounter** anyway as, just at that moment, Mrs Randall, our **headmistress** grabs my poor hand. She starts talking at me loudly about the *Queen Mother's* ***generous*** *contribution to Chalk Farm School* blah blah and her very "generous" hat totally blocks my view of Nora and Miss Bardwell.

By the time Mrs Randall has *finally* moved along the line to my mother and I **glance** over towards Nora, I realise that I've missed all the action. Nora looks like she's been hit by a bus. And guess who was driving that bus, kids?

Miss Bardwell, **aka** "The bus driver", has finished saying something probably awful, and is turning to move away, **heading towards** a taxi that seems to be waiting for her (and Mrs Randall and Mrs Randall's hat, who are both making their way to the taxi, too.) Nora stares after Miss Bardwell for a moment before suddenly **cutting across** the **cemetery** in the direction of her **trusty** old Citroën. She doesn't even glance back at us.

Hmm, **yummy**, pie finished, flashback over. And as I said, that scene has been bothering me ever since. Nora had seemed fairly together before she met Miss Bardwell. She had seemed to have her grief in control. But ever since *The Scene in the* ***Churchyard***, it's like she's on Planet

+++ encounter – Zusammentreffen +++ headmistress – Rektorin +++ generous – großzügig +++ to glance – schauen +++ aka – alias +++ to head towards – zugehen auf +++ to cut across s.th. – quer über etw. gehen +++ cemetery – Friedhof +++ trusty – treu +++ yummy – lecker +++ churchyard – Friedhof +++

Pain or something. Talking to her over the past few days has been like trying to eat a sandwich still in its plastic **wrapper** – difficult.

I'm *dying* to know what was said at the funeral, not just because I care about my aunt but also because I care about myself. Miss Bardwell has such an influence on my life at Chalk Farm School. I need to know.

I say, expectantly, wiping my mouth, "Nora, you have to tell me. What did Miss Bardwell say to you at the funeral?"

It's as though I accidentally wiped the smile from her face at the same time as I wiped the **crumbs** from my face. Nora says a bit coldly, "You're quite sure you want to know? It will only make things more complicated."

Ooh, complications, I *love* them. Sometimes it seems like my whole London life has just been one *giant* complication. "Bring it on," I say, my teeth **gritted**. *Bring it on.*

+++ wrapper – Verpackung +++ crumb – Krümel +++
to grit one's teeth – die Zähne zusammenbeißen +++

Nora Brings It On

Nora hesitates but not for long. She wants to tell me, I know it. "Oh, it was pretty much your standard condolence speech. I believe Connie's exact words to me were that I was always such a disappointment to my mother! I was always so selfish and so **vain**. Mother knew I never really loved her. And ..." – Nora looks uncertain again for a moment, then **steels herself** – "taking Miss Bardwell's fiancé away was **the final straw** for my mother. It was the shame of that which ... killed her."

Nora has gone pale just repeating what Miss Bardwell said. Her right hand has left the pile of letters and has **wound** itself tightly around a **strand** of her long, blonde hair. Still, she actually manages to smile.

My mouth is hanging open. I must look really unattractive, bits of pie crust flying out, probably.

Nora politely ignores the pie chaos around my mouth and goes on, "The worst thing is ... Connie was right. I *was* a disappointment to my mother, no question. I never

+++ vain – eitel +++ to steel oneself – all seinen Mut zusammennehmen +++ the final straw – der Tropfen, der das Fass zum Überlaufen bringt +++ to wound – (sich) winden +++ strand – Strähne +++

had a family, I never played by any of her rules, I never showed her enough respect."

"Nonsense!" I say furiously. Oh, I'm so angry with Miss Bardwell I could ***crush*** what's left of this delicious apple pie with my fist! I'm trying to think of something **supportive** to say to Nora when she suddenly gets to her feet. "I have to get on," she says. She picks up her letters and looks at me sternly: "Promise me you won't tell anyone about this. Not Sam, no one. And try not to **obsess about** what Bardwell said. She's just a bitter, sad, lonely woman."

It's possible that I nod when Nora says: *don't obsess*. But you know, I'm quite sure that you know, I now have a new goal. For saying what she did to my aunt, at her mother's funeral, Miss Bardwell must pay. She will pay.

Before I can obsess about that – sorry Nora! – it's time to say goodbye to Sam. We turn down Nora's offer of a **lift** and my mother's offer to pay for a taxi and decide that we will **indeed** walk together to the local train station. From there, Sam will get a train back to London, where he'll get the coach to Glasgow. He should be home by next Wednesday! Joke! Seriously, it is a *long* journey.

Sam says a quick goodbye to my parents – who are obviously still **astonished** that he said no to the Queen Mother's cash – and then we **set off** on our long trek to the railway station. It's about three kilometres, in fact, so

+++ to crush – zerquetschen +++ supportive – unterstützend +++ to obsess about s.th. – sich in etw. hineinsteigern +++ lift – Mitfahrgelegenheit +++ indeed – wirklich +++ astonished – erstaunt +++ to set off – aufbrechen +++

it will take us a good hour but we both want the time to talk. I've brought my new camera with me, too, to show Sam. I'm very proud of it. I still can't quite believe it's nearly mine: at least it will be when I've finished paying the friend of Nora's that I'm buying it from.

I feel really **disloyal** to my old camera, which will be sitting sadly by itself in my **dorm** back at Chalk Farm, while I'm out here "dating" my new one. But anyway, the new camera's an absolute **cracker**, a really excellent digital one, **state of the art**. Nora gave it to me on the morning of Grandma's funeral. I've been desperate to try it out and now I take a few shots of Sam. I want to remember

+++ disloyal – untreu +++ dorm – Schlafsaal +++ cracker – Knüller +++ state of the art – hochmodern +++

Sam coming here, remember how much I once meant to him. I **caption** the photos in my head: *The end of the line.*

We talk about a few final things on the way. I explain a bit more about Sebastian and the letter that I wrote Sam, explaining everything, the one that got sent back to me. I tell him all about how I'll go to work at *The Sentinel*, the newspaper where Nora works at weekends. Again, the **implication** is clear: I'll be doing that every Saturday so there will be no time to go up to Scotland.

Sam, being a nice guy, simply wishes me luck at *The Sentinel* and gives me a quick kiss. I can't help but notice that he doesn't look back as he walks along the train **carriage** looking for a seat. Ouch. I take a photo of the train, **pulling** out of the station, then delete it. It's too sad. Oooh, digital cameras! It's quite fun deleting pictures, actually.

+++ to caption – beschriften +++ implication – Schlussfolgerung +++ carriage – Waggon +++ to pull – *hier:* fahren +++

I Can See Clearly Now …

I'll tell you something that isn't sad, though: it's amazing. I can't wait to get back to London and for the first time, it's not because a boy is waiting for me. It's the thought of working at *The Sentinel.*

I leave for London with Nora the day after Sam. My parents and Max will stay on a bit longer at The Grange with Dieter (who doesn't seem to have anything else to do), "putting my grandmother's **affairs** in order". I know Nora and my mother have to decide what will happen with Grandma's house, which was left to both of them. They will sell it, probably, though they might think about **renting** it **out**. "Luxusprobleme," says my father, as he kisses me goodbye. "Wir sind reich, mein Schatz, wer hätte so was geglaubt?" Dad looks a bit **miserable** about it. Maybe it's the old socialist in him. "Dieser Sam ist ein guter Junge," he says thoughtfully. I'm noticing that people love integrity! I must get myself some!

Nora and me drive into London in her Citroën. It might be the last time I'm ever in this cool car, I think sadly. Maybe Nora's thinking about that too; anyway, we

+++ affair – Angelegenheit +++ to rent out – vermieten +++ miserable – unglücklich +++

don't say much to each other. My head, which is usually as **muddled** and **dizzy** as that of someone who's just spent a week chained to a *Kinderkarussel*, today feels as clear as crystal, thank you very much. Death does that to people, I've heard. Gives you **priorities**.

I haven't felt this determined in my life before. As Nora and me drive through London, on this **crisp** autumn day, the city finally **makes sense** to me, perfect sense. I suddenly know why I'm here. I'm not here boy hunting. I'm here to get an education. I'm here to improve my photography skills. I'm here to get the most of my experience at *The Sentinel*.

Nora drops me at the tube station nearest my school. (My idea, to avoid Miss Bardwell.) "I'll see you at the paper next Saturday," she smiles, **pecking** me on the cheek. "Don't be too nervous!"

I won't. It's the new me, remember? As I stand in the doorway of the school, **underneath** its red **brick** towers, I might look like the same person who arrived here just over a year ago. I still have the same hair (I fear I will always have the same boring hair). I'm the same **height** that I was then (**give or take one centimetre**), the same weight (give or take one or two plates of chips). But actually, I've **shed** a skin, like a snake. I'm stronger, sadder and badder. And I **intend** to make my grandmother proud.

+++ muddled – durcheinander +++ dizzy – schwindelig +++ priority – Priorität +++ crisp – frisch +++ to make sense – Sinn ergeben +++ to peck – flüchtig küssen +++ underneath – unter +++ brick – Ziegelstein +++ height – Größe +++ give or take one centimetre – ein Zentimeter hin oder her +++ to shed – *hier:* abwerfen +++ to intend – vorhaben +++

When I finally walk into History later, it's a bit like one of those scenes in Westerns when a mysterious stranger wanders over to the bar in a saloon: everyone stops talking. I don't think it's because I look different, skinless and **mean**. I know it's because everyone has heard about my grandmother. Everyone knows everything about each other at Chalk Farm – **bra** size, shoe size, mother's middle name – so it's no surprise. Becks, my roommate, was also at Grandma's funeral … oh, here's Becks now, coming towards me, looking worried.

She's a **giant** of a girl, Becks, with muscles like those early pictures of Arnold Schwarzenegger, before he was governor of California, when he was just good old Mr Olympia. She has a heart the same size as her **pecs**, luckily.

"How are you, Emily?" she says, in what in Becksland is probably a whisper but which still seems to make the walls of our beloved school shake.

"OK," I mutter. "Thanks again for coming to the funeral, Becks …"

I'm interrupted. It's Melissa and Sadie, the other two inmates of Cell 3B, with long faces. "We're really sorry about your grandmother," says Melissa and Sadie mumbles, "Yes, awful …"

I'm going to hear the same things repeated over and over again, I know it. Luckily, I can **rely on** one person not to be boringly kind. Somewhere, towards the window side of the classroom, I hear it: "Big deal, so her *grand-*

+++ mean – gemein +++ bra – BH +++ giant – Riese +++ pecs – Brustmuskeln +++ to rely on s.b. – sich auf jmdn. verlassen +++

mother died. Look at her, you can tell she's *loving* the attention." Ah, **Cyclops**. I can tell she's going to be my **rock** at this difficult time.

I really don't care about Cyclops Dobson right now. That's the best thing about not sharing a dorm with her as I did before. I don't *have to* care about her any more. And right now, I have to save my energy for Miss Bardwell. Speak of the devil.

Miss Bardwell's head has suddenly appeared around the door of our classroom. Someone screams. It is indeed a horrible sight. "Emily!" Miss Bardwell's head says sharply. "May I speak to you for a moment?" The head nods in the direction of the corridor.

I don't move. I don't want to speak to Miss Bardwell's head – or to any other part of her. Finally, the mountain comes to Mohammed: Miss Bardwell enters the room and **approaches** my desk. She's **annoyed** with me. I've double-**dissed** her: I didn't come over to her and I know too that I should have reported to her when I came back into school. I just couldn't be bothered.

"Emily, I wanted to see how you were. I wasn't aware that you were back in school?"

It's an accusation, of course, and my **cue** to say: *Sorry Miss!* but instead, I just shrug. It's **rude**, I know it but – hey! – telling someone that they murdered their mother *at their mother's own funeral* is also a tiny bit impolite, wouldn't you say so?

+++ Cyclops – Zyklop +++ rock – *hier ironisch:* Fels in der Brandung +++ to approach – zukommen auf +++ annoyed – verärgert +++ to diss – *hier:* missachten +++ cue – Stichwort +++ rude – unhöflich +++

Miss Bardwell folds her arms across her **bony chest.** "I've been worried about you, naturally, as your housemistress and a close friend of the family."

I can't help it, I just laugh. I actually laugh out loud. A friend to our family? The Millington-Hausmann family has **genetic disorders** running in it that are better "friends". Miss Bardwell looks **uneasy**. She glances in Cyclops' direction, obviously **seeking** support. She's unsure of herself. She's wondering if Nora told me what she said, I suppose. Well, good.

The situation is getting more and more **awkward**. Miss Bardwell is still standing above me now but all I can see is her **waist** and her legs. I haven't made eye contact with her once. The room is completely silent again, I notice, just like it was when I came in. No one is reviewing their homework on 14th century farming techniques, I'm sure, and *everyone* is watching Bardwell and me.

I ignore Miss Bardwell completely. I get out my textbook. I open my **jotter**. I look at my pen carefully. I don't look at her. *She simply isn't there.*

Finally, I hear her say, "Well, if you want to talk about anything, you know where I am."

That's when I do look up. I **raise** my head and stare at Miss Bardwell, straight in her coal-black eyes. I say, "Yes, I know where to find you."

Cyclops takes a sharp intake of breath.

+++ bony – knochig +++ chest – Brust +++ genetic disorder – genetische Störung +++ uneasy – unbehaglich +++ to seek – suchen +++ awkward – unangenehm +++ waist – Taille +++ jotter – Notizblock +++ to raise – heben +++

Melissa and Sadie tell me later, **breathlessly**, that it *totally, absolutely* did sound like a **threat** when I said it. *I know where to find you.* I'm not even sure that I *meant* to threaten Miss Bardwell but anyway, good. If that's what Miss Bardwell thinks it was, I mean it: *good.*

The girls are a bit shocked. As we do the *Obduktion* on What Happened Today in History back in the dorm later, it's clear that Melissa, Becks and Sadie don't quite understand why I was so rude to Miss Bardwell before. They know that I don't like her – no one except Amanda actually *likes* her. But everyone knows that you don't **cross** Miss Bardwell, not if you want to live. Melissa tells me quietly, "You know, she might be ***genuinely*** worried about you. She actually asked us all to pray for you and your grandmother, you know."

I sigh. I don't want to hear this right now. I can't tell the girls what Miss Bardwell said to Nora. So I just shrug and say, "She doesn't care about me, trust me." Sadie sighs and Melissa sighs and Becks finally also decides to sigh. "Well, you have to decide," says Melissa finally. "But maybe it's best not to get on the wrong side of her …"

Then Melissa tells me that Miss Bardwell has been pretty nasty to them in class over the past couple of days. "She even made Tracy cry! It was horrible: Tracy couldn't think of the right answer and Miss Bardwell just wouldn't leave her alone. She told Tracy she was a **disgrace** to the school. I don't think her **sabbatical** has changed her."

+++ breathless – atemlos +++ threat – (Be-)Drohung +++ to cross s.b. – jmdn. verärgern +++ genuine – echt, ehrlich +++ disgrace – Schande +++ sabbatical – unbezahlter Urlaub +++

Miss Bardwell disappeared suddenly to a spiritual **retreat** in Japan last **term**, after her break-up with Mr Michaels. She had been looking for "inner peace", but: she should ask that holiday company for her money back.

I'm tired, after all the **tension** and all the travelling today, but it's clear that I will *have to* meet Maudie and Kim, my best friends here at Chalk Farm School. They're in a different house – Bloomsbury, so I don't have classes with them. I'm actually not very **keen** to get together with them tonight. I don't want to discuss the funeral or how I'm feeling again but the girls, **bless** them, won't give me any peace until they've seen with their own eyes that I'm still alive, it seems.

So I drag my **weary** bones down to White Out, our favourite café and meeting place, later on that evening. Maudie and Kim are waiting for me and when I arrive, they **hug** me, a bit tearfully. Mrs White, the owner's wife, built like a garage, rushes over to join us. "I heard about your granny, dearie," she blubbers. "Everything's on the house tonight." Then she hurries away again to get our usual orders of chips and tea.

Maudie and Kim look at me blankly: "I've no idea how she knows!" Maudie says slowly.

"Although I have had the feeling before that Mrs White listens to our conversations," whispers Kim. "Do you know what I mean?"

+++ retreat – Rückzug +++ term – Schulhalbjahr +++ tension – Anspannung +++ to be keen – begeistert sein +++ bless them – die Guten +++ weary – müde, erschöpft +++ to hug – umarmen +++

I do. Still, at least no privacy means free chips! Mrs White comes over with them and after I've eaten a couple, I feel a bit livelier. I tell the girls all about the funeral, though not the bit about Nora and Miss Bardwell, much as I would love to. I do tell the girls about Sam arriving to see me and about Grandma's will, of course. They can't believe that Sam turned down the Queen Mother's offer to come back to London.

"Wow," said Maudie, **shuffling** a particularly big chip round her mouth. "Oh, ooh, these are hot!" she **squeals**. "That shows real integrity. He's one in a million Sam, isn't he?" See what I mean? Integrity. Make a note of it.

+++ to shuffle – *hier:* schieben +++ to squeal – kreischen +++

Kim nods **eagerly**, shaking her baby blonde hair a little. "**Fancy** coming all that way to see you and then walking away from the money! It's like something someone would do in a film, you know, like a James Stewart or a Gregory Peck character." She loves old movies, Kim, and it's no **coincidence** that her boyfriend, Jonathan, looks like he stepped off the set of a Fred Astaire film or something.

Then Maudie says seriously, "But what does that mean for you two?"

The girls know all about my relationship crisis. **Heck**, these girls could take a **GCSE** in Problems in Emily Hausmann's Love Life. They certainly know Sam and me were having a hard time. They definitely know that I thought I might be in love with Sebastian Junger.

It seems so stupid now. Sam versus Sebastian, it's a **no-brainer**. Sam is so much cooler. Sebastian didn't even reply to my text message telling him that my grandmother had died. Nice.

Even so, I know there's no future for Sam and me and that's exactly what I tell Maudie and Kim. "It's pretty much over," I say quietly, trying very hard not to let Mrs White hear me. She's wiping one of the tables near us right now and she really does seem to be trying to listen in!

Maudie, Kim and Mrs White look sad, genuinely sad. Maudie says, sighing, "It's not easy, the whole long-distance relationship thing, is it?"

+++ eager – eifrig +++ fancy – *hier:* nicht zu fassen +++ coincidence – Zufall +++ heck – Mist! +++ GCSE – Schulabschluss +++ it's a no-brainer – *hier:* das ist kein Vergleich +++

Maudie doesn't quite say, *Thank goodness my boyfriend is here in London!* but it's written all over her face. Maudie is dating Matt, Sam's friend and the bass player in the Kitty Gagarins, our very own personal "boy pool", it seems!

The really strange thing is that I actually don't feel jealous right now – not of Maudie, nor Kim, nor Mrs White, who's now cuddling her ex-boxer husband Mr White. I *was* jealous, very much so, just a few weeks ago, of anyone in the world who had a boyfriend they could see regularly. But the feeling has just stopped. Something in me just isn't that interested in being close to a boy right now. No, I don't want to lie down. I don't want to see a doctor.

I *do want* to see how Miss Bardwell will behave with me the next time I have a class with her, which is on Thursday. But on Thursday, Miss Bardwell **has other fish to fry**, it seems. She has an announcement to make. She's so excited about it that she seems to have forgotten about me completely.

She stands in front of us, her fourth form Latin class, beaming. She's actually wearing a shirt that has, like, a *pattern* on it today. It's just a pattern of very tiny dots but still, it tells us that "Miss" is definitely in a good mood.

"Ladies," she cries. "You've all heard the sad news that Carol Byrne will be leaving our school." Miss Bardwell smiles broadly. She's not sad at all, even though the word on the street is that Carol's parents can't afford to pay for Chalk Farm any more.

+++ to have other fish to fry – Wichtigeres zu tun haben +++

I'm trying to work out why Carol Byrne leaving is worth an announcement. Carol is in the year above us in the fifth form, so most of us don't know her very well. And then it all makes sense. Then we find out the reason for the patterned shirt: Carol is a ***prefect***.

Prefects. You might not know anything about prefects. If so, you're lucky. Prefects are pupils who are given special "powers" and "duties". They are the beautiful people, the chosen ones. They get to wear **badges** and – ooh – special gold **braiding** on their blazers and tell other girls what to do. They get all the best jobs after school, someone told me. Some of them are actually OK, some of them are a **nightmare**.

"... so with Carol *sadly* leaving, this means that we shall have to elect a new prefect. Normally, we select girls from the fifth form but as the school year has already begun anyway, we've decided therefore to allow the fourth form to choose their very own prefect!" Miss Bardwell claps her hands and squeals!

Wow. I yawn. I couldn't care less if I tried. Prefect elections are always a stupid popularity **contest**, of course. Although someone did tell me that the elections in our house, Kensington, are about as democratic as those in North Korea. The girls that become prefects are always, always "Kim Jong Bardill's" favourites and ...

Oh, I get it! A light bulb finally appears above my stupid head. Miss Bardwell is smiling at Amanda. She might

+++ prefect – Vertrauensschüler/in +++ badge – Abzeichen +++ braid(ing) – Borte +++ nightmare – Albtraum +++ contest – Wettbewerb +++

as well say, *There will be one* **vacancy** *for Amanda to become a prefect.* There's no point in voting: the result is in the bag. Amanda "Cyclops" Dobson will be adding that gold braid to her blazer, no matter how many **votes** she actually gets. I know it. I suddenly see Amanda before my eyes in her prefect's blazer, ordering me to clean the toilets with my hair. There's no way I'm going to let it happen. No way I'm going to be policed by Amanda.

And suddenly I realise too: this is it. I've been looking for a battlefield on which to fight with Miss Bardwell and I think I may just have found it.

I feel much happier than I did when I walked into this room. I've just **spotted** an amazing window of opportunity. It's perfect: what would annoy Miss Bardwell more than anything? The answer is easy: *if someone she didn't like won the prefect election.*

I'm the most obvious candidate, of course. Miss Bardwell really doesn't like me. There's just one problem: I don't want to be a prefect. If I actually won the election, it would mean spending my time watching the queues at lunchtime and reporting to Bardwell. **Not on your nelly**.

I look round me **frantically**. I gaze at the faces of my classmates, wondering how much Miss Bardwell hates them. Hmmm, there's Becks. Miss Bardwell certainly doesn't *love* Becks, but I'm not sure she really *dislikes* her either. Becks would never agree to be a prefect anyway.

+++ vacancy – freie Stelle +++ vote – Wahl, Stimme +++ to spot – entdecken +++ not on your nelly – nie im Leben +++ frantic – verzweifelt +++

She'd never do anything that reduced her time for sport. There's Tracy, no, she'd be too scared … Oh, hello! Sadie! Of course! Sadie, my roommate, would be a perfect prefect. Miss Bardwell seems to be **offended** by Sadie's **very** existence. Sadie's not pretty or clever or *schleimig*. She's dreamy and pleasant and **lacks confidence**, all qualities that Miss Bardwell hates. I watch Sadie now, polishing her glasses and laughing at something to herself. She looks a bit **loopy**, right now, it has to be said. Perfect!

Oh I could hug myself – I'm a political genius. I've got the dream candidate – the anti-Amanda. I smile all the way through Miss Bardwell's description of the voting procedure for the prefects. It's ridiculous. What Bardwell would love to say is: *Put a cross next to Amanda's name or else* … She can't, of course, so instead she says things like: *You might want to consider students who have overcome* ***adversity***. She looks meaningfully at Cyclops while Cyclops lowers her head, sorrowfully.

Bardwell's talking about Amanda's accident, of course, when a hockey ball mistook her **eye socket** for a goal three years ago. Ever since then she's had one eye bigger than the other. It can look a bit creepy if you get her at a certain **angle**; you don't see it at all from others. My candidate can beat that anyway: she's a born underdog, Sadie. And, as anybody who watches any of those TV talent shows will tell you – *everyone loves an underdog*.

+++ offended – gekränkt +++ very – *hier:* pur +++ to lack confidence – kein Selbstvertrauen haben +++ loopy – verrückt +++ adversity – Unglück +++ eye socket – Augenhöhle +++ angle – Winkel +++

Like the Titanic to the Iceberg

Good, good, good: I have a plan. There's still the small matter of actually *telling* Sadie that she's a prefect candidate, but I'll give her the good news later. Now, it's only one day until I start at *The Sentinel* and I need to concentrate on getting ready for that.

I spend all of Friday night in front of one of the school's computers, with a packet of dry roasted **peanuts** and a bottle of Coke, researching the newspaper and trying to find out something about **digital imaging**. I even MSN Sam for some tips on computers: Sam's a computer **whiz**. People may laugh at computer whizzes, aka **geeks**, but right now I'd give anything to be one.

Sam is no help. He just keeps digitally "laughing" and writing things like: "You! Working with computers!" And: "Remember: if your computer stops working, try switching it on and off again. Or try **plugging it in**."

Computer humour. How funny it is. He sounds happy, Sam, I have to say, really happy. We MSN for a bit more but neither of us mentions meeting up with each other

+++ peanut – Erdnuss +++ digital imaging – digitale Bildverarbeitung +++ whiz – Genie, Ass +++ geek – Außenseiter/in +++ to plug in – einstecken +++

again. It's a **relief** not to have to try. We still haven't officially split up, of course. I suppose we really should. That's something else that will have to wait until after this weekend. Right now, I need to get onto Wikipedia … what year was *The Sentinel* **founded** again?

1876! It employs 1,009 people! It has the largest circulation in London! On Friday night, I dream facts about *The Sentinel.* My head is still **buzzing** when I enter its building early, really early, on Saturday morning. The reception area is beautiful: with huge high **ceilings**, white walls and chairs **shaped** like surrealist Salvador Dali lips, in bright colours. There are four bouquets of fresh flowers – four! – on the reception desk, one for each smiling receptionist. I tell one of them, a beautiful looking red-haired woman, what I'm here for and she nods, checks on the computer and then gives me my very own identification card.

Then I sit nervously on a pair of **fuchsia** lips, watching a giant plasma TV screen on the wall. It's showing pictures of recent events and reporting some of the headlines of the day. More bank trouble. Yawn. Like I said, it's frighteningly early: 6.40 am. I think it's safe to say I've never been up this early at the weekend in my life before. I could **murder** a coffee though I'm not sure where to get one.

I'm to wait for Nora here in reception and we'll go up

+++ relief – Erleichterung +++ to found – gründen +++ to buzz – summen +++ ceiling – Decke +++ shaped – geformt +++ fuchsia – bestimmter Rotton +++ to murder – *hier:* vernichten +++

together to the "morning conference". This is where the **editor-in-chief** of *The Sentinel* will discuss the big stories of the day and tell everyone what to focus on. It's all completely **terrifying**, frankly. I'm just about to sit in on a conference in one of the most important national newspapers in the United Kingdom. My heart feels like it's made of **semtex**. And I really don't want to be late. The conference starts at 7.00 and there's no sign of Nora yet.

We joke a lot in our family about my Auntie Nora being late for everything. I've often wondered whether she's also always late for work. The answer it seems is *no* as here she is now, at 6.48 am, a whole magical twelve

+++ editor-in-chief – Chefredakteur/in +++ terrifying – Angst einflößend +++ semtex – Sprengstoff +++

minutes early. Did you get that last word? EARLY. It's true. Nora really is only late when she's meeting her loved ones. Brilliant. Makes me feel all warm and special.

Nora comes over to greet me: she also looks tired and is carrying two bucket-sized cups of coffee in her hands. She passes one to me, smiling: "Thought you might need this. Nervous?"

It's quite a stupid question really, isn't it? Nora smiles and **squeezes** my arm. "They'll love you." Then she **winks** at a security guard and the two of us go up together in the glass lift. The conference room is on the fourth floor.

PING! Here we are! Personally, I had always imagined that a newspaper's offices would be grey and serious. Well, it's the news, isn't it? It is *serious, grey* stuff. But when we step out onto the fourth floor, I see that it's like the lobby, a **riot** of colour. It feels more like a funky "lounge" bar than a paper here. You almost expect to see people **clutching** glasses of caipirinha walking around.

There are groups of brightly-coloured retro-style chairs everywhere and even – get this! – "Fat Boys"! Nora tells me that these are called the "breakout areas". "The news room gets totally crazy and these are supposed to be spaces where we can relax a bit." She hesitates. "And sleep! You'll always see someone who's just passed out on one of the bean bags after a night **shift** or when we've covered a really big story. 9/11 was totally crazy, there were people asleep everywhere in the days after that."

I'm an idiot, of course, but it still seems a bit weird,

to squeeze – drücken +++ to wink – zwinkern +++ riot – *hier:* Durcheinander +++ to clutch – halten +++ shift – Schicht +++

frankly: thinking about how to cover a terrible terrorist attack while sitting on a bean bag or a bright pink pair of giant lips. I suppose it might keep you **sane**. Or drive you mad. I can't quite decide.

Nora takes me first past the newsroom, which is already full of people sitting behind computer screens, shouting at each other. Ooh, it's just like it is in the movies! The hand holding my coffee is shaking with excitement while my face is trying to play it cool. Like I've been in a million newsrooms before.

We finally reach the conference room, which is already **fairly** full. Everyone, really, everyone, nods and smiles at Nora. She's just starting to introduce me to a couple of people when a tall, thin man of about 50 with glasses and black hair enters the room and calls for everyone's attention. Nora **nudges** me: *Russell, the editor-in-chief.* I nod. I knew that actually – I googled him last night, too! I'm a brilliant investigative reporter!

Russell starts talking quickly, almost too quickly for me to follow, about what's happening in the world. I was right – it's mainly problems at banks. An **earthquake** in Honduras. A few of the other chief reporters speak. Then Russell says, "Lastly, we have a couple of young people who will be spending some time with us. Nora? Where is she?"

Nora grins and points at me and I blush, right on cue. Russell smiles warmly. "Yes, we have a real live Berliner in the room. This is Nora's **niece**, Emily Hausmann."

+++ sane – bei Verstand +++ fairly – ziemlich +++ to nudge – anstoßen +++ earthquake – Erdbeben +++ niece – Nichte +++

Someone **snorts**. *Hey!* It seems like the sound came from one young man, with a **beard** and carrying a laptop. He's rolling his eyes and looking cross. *What did I do?*

"... I hear Emily's a talented photographer herself," Russell continues, (SNORT!) "and she'll be helping out in the art department at weekends."

Then Russell turns to face the snorting man. "And we finally also get the chance to welcome Chris Morris today, winner of our Young Journalist competition. Chris was supposed to start with us on Monday but has been ill." – Should I snort here, too, I wonder? – "He'll be with us for the next three months. Welcome on board!"

Everyone smiles happily at Chris, who only manages a very miserable smile back. He really is a very serious-looking young man indeed. He doesn't look that young, actually. He's sort of good-looking, no doubt, if you're into older guys. (I am not. No way. I do not, repeat do not, have anything like a Daddy complex. **The thought**.)

I'm still wondering about the snort, of course. I'm sure the **implication** is clear – Chris *won a competition*! He's a great young talent who beat thousands of others to be here! And me? I'm a stupid little girl, who's standing here because my mum happens to be the sister of a top photographer.

If that's really what Chris is thinking, he's absolutely right, of course.

+++ to snort – schnauben, prusten +++ beard – Bart +++ The thought. – Allein der Gedanke. +++ implication – *hier:* Bedeutung +++

Apart from Chris being a bit unfriendly, the rest of the day at *The Sentinel* is just great, almost perfect. After morning conference, I'm taken by the art director, a man named Todd, who Nora tells me is a "sweetheart", to see how his department works. He introduces me to graphic designers, IT guys and the photographers, all of whom are warm and friendly and do not snort at or near me.

In fact, I have such a great, interesting morning that I've almost forgotten about Chris. I don't think about him at all until I'm queuing up later in the canteen. *The Sentinel* canteen is **gorgeous**, on the top floor of the building, with what they always call "**stunning** views" over the Thames. I'm feeling **suitably** stunned and helping myself at the salad bar when I spot Chris. He's sitting by himself, peering at his laptop and eating what looks like a hamburger at the same time. Everything about him – *everything* – says: *I am busy and important.* ***Leave me alone.*** *Do not come and sit next to me.*

I can't help it. I'm just drawn towards him, like the Titanic towards the iceberg. Like I said, it's been a perfect day. The only thing that wasn't perfect was the way Chris snorted at me. Or did I imagine it? I'd love to know for sure. And we're the new kids on the block anyway; we should talk to each other.

So I take my tray and I sail over to sit down opposite to Chris. He doesn't look up at first, he just smiles absently. I wait for a moment, then say brightly, "Hello! I'm Emily."

+++ gorgeous – wunderschön +++ stunning – überwältigend +++ suitable – angemessen +++ to leave s.b. alone – jmdn. in Ruhe lassen +++

Chris finally raises his eyes from his computer screen. He's got a Mac, of course, he is *soooo* a Mac guy! Anyway, there's now no doubt: I didn't imagine it. His face falls. His face falls so hard, in fact, it must have dropped right down to the ground floor. He'll have to pick it up later in reception.

Sitting down here was definitely a really bad idea but I'm stuck now, of course. All I can do is try to be friendly. Maybe if I can now show Chris the real me, he'll realise that I'm not some **posh** snob who's just **lucked** her way **in** here. Yeah. Maybe.

Chris is now just staring at the "real me", still **frowning**. He has his **sleeves** rolled up, I notice, and **yikes**! He has incredibly hairy arms. Unbelievable.

"How was it then?" I mumble. "Your first day …"

Chris doesn't reply at once. I do believe that he's wondering if it would totally ruin his career chances to ignore me. Maybe he's thinking that I will tell my aunt that he was rude to me. He finally says, "Fine."

That's all he says. *Fine.*

He doesn't say, *And yours, Emily? Thanks for coming over to talk to me. I was lonely before.* It's hopeless. I'll have one last final shot and then I'll crawl back over to the salad bar and try and **drown myself** in the **garlic** sauce or something. This is *sooooo* embarrassing.

I start to try and formulate an intelligent question and

+++ posh – vornehm, reich +++ to luck in s.th. – durch Glück an etw. kommen +++ to frown – die Stirn runzeln +++ sleeve – Ärmel +++ yikes – du lieber Himmel +++ to drown oneself – sich ertränken +++ garlic – Knoblauch +++

then something awful happens. My intelligent question comes out in a horrible German accent: "Vot kind of zings are you doing here?"

Don't get me wrong. I'm not saying that the German accent *itself* is horrible but, man, mine is. It's a weird tic I have: whenever I'm really nervous, my English goes all super comedy-German on me. **I keep meaning to** google my "illness" – there must be some support group for bilingual idiots like me who can't keep their accents straight.

But – a miracle! – it's very strange. My German accent seems to get Chris's interest. He says, as though remembering it for the first time, "You're from Berlin, did Russell say?" I love being a Berliner. You're automatically cool. It opens so many doors. All the world is your friend when you're from Berlin.

"Yes," I say. Well, it's true. Now's probably not the time to tell Chris that I'm currently at a posh girls' school in Camden. So I don't. Let him imagine that I'm Rosa Luxemburg or whatever it is he associates with Berlin.

"Cool," says Chris. He looks at me carefully. He's obviously trying to decide if he should **change his mind** about me or not. Then he remembers my first question, luckily, and starts to tell me *everything* he did today. He was working in the news room and he's totally excited about some story that they're covering which *I know nothing about.*

He can certainly talk about the news, Chris, boy oh

+++ to keep meaning to do s.th. – schon immer etw. tun wollen +++ to change one's mind – seine Meinung ändern +++

boy. What he can't do is small talk: during the next 20 minutes or so, all I learn about Chris is that he's at journalism college, he's from Newcastle and he wants nothing more – and nothing else, it seems – than to be a reporter, a real old-school investigative reporter.

"If there are still newspapers around in a few years," he says **gloomily**. "I mean, what with the *revolution in media platforms ... paywalls ... new media ... transformative technology*." I nod hard. I'll be up all night finding out what these things are!

Chris does talk about one thing that I actually know something about: blogs. He has his own one. Ever since I had that "experience" with Ed Stanton, the word "blog" has been a dirty one for me, but Chris talks about his own with such passion that I find myself **copying down** the link for it.

Passionate. That's the word to describe him. **Obsessive**, even. Definitely **driven**. And he definitely takes himself far too seriously.

Chris finally looks at the time on his laptop and says, "Have to get back." He frowns for a minute and then says slowly, "Nice talking to you."

I'm not really sure he means it. But I hope at least I've convinced him that I'm human.

The rest of the day flies past. I'm so sad when it's over I could cry. I feel like screaming: Let me move in here! Let

+++ gloomy – bedrückt +++ to copy down – aufschreiben +++ obsessive – bessessen +++ driven – ehrgeizig +++

me sleep on a Fat Boy and eat in the canteen every day! I totally could. *The Sentinel* is *soooo* cool.

The whole day has made me feel incredibly motivated, actually. If there was any doubt in my mind before, now I'm totally sure. I really want to work in photo-journalism. But I know I have so much work to do. I have to get used to digital photography! No more retro-style shots! I have to get "into" computers! I sigh. Sam would laugh so hard, if he heard that. I'm not really technically **gifted**. On the other hand, everyone has to start somewhere. So even though the teacher, Mr Thornton, is apparently really creepy, I'm still definitely going to sign up for computer studies next term, definitely.

I'm tired when I get back to school but I still force myself to head straight to one of the computer rooms again. Firstly, I want to see what's in the online edition of *The Sentinel*. And, well, secondly, I have to confess that I'm curious to see Chris's blog.

I'm slightly worried too. Like I said, I've been the victim of "blog **abuse**" before and I don't **fancy** having it happen again. But Chris's blog is all excited stuff about some of the things he talked about before that I don't know anything about. He doesn't even mention me, which is good, of course. Isn't it?

I sleep for nearly all of Sunday and before I know it, it's Monday again, and back on the **chain gang**. The new serious me is starting to realise that I have to decide *where* to

+++ gifted – begabt +++ abuse – Missbrauch +++ to fancy – gern mögen +++ chain gang – Sträflingskolonne

get serious. If I'm going to use my grandmother's money to stay at Chalk Farm school, I'm going to have exams here soon – GCSEs – and I'm going to study hard for them. And if I don't want to finish school here in London, then I had better get back to Germany *ganz schnell.* They'll also start studying towards the *Abitur* soon as Betti and Merle, my friends back in Berlin, are always telling me.

I decide I'd better go and talk to Miss Shaw about things. Miss Shaw is wonderful, our totally cool art teacher. She's always been very supportive of me and right now, I urgently need some **career advice**.

When I meet Miss Shaw in her classroom later to tell her about my dilemma, she's as lovely as ever and very understanding. She asks what I would like to do in the future and, embarrassed, I tell her that I'd like to do a photo-journalism course.

She smiles. "How nice!" She tells me all about some of the great art colleges in Britain. "There's a very good one in Glasgow!" she says with a **cheeky grin** – does she really know about Sam?

But Miss Shaw also says that there's a lot of competition for places on these courses. If I really want to go to one of the better art schools, I would indeed be best to start concentrating now. It's never too early to start putting together a **decent portfolio**. She hesitates. "Are you planning to stay on at school here in London or not Emily?"

"I, erm, I don't know, Miss," I say, hanging my head. I

+++ career advice – Berufsberatung +++ cheeky – frech +++ grin – Grinsen +++ decent – ordentlich +++ portfolio – Mappe +++

hate that question. Up till now I've just sort of hoped that falling in love with a boy would answer it for me. It's really clear that policy hasn't worked for me.

We talk through my options. Miss Shaw thinks if I definitely don't want to complete my education in London, I should return to Berlin at the end of this term. "Otherwise I imagine you'll be out of touch with the German education system. And **vice versa**, there's no point in **getting all caught up in** GCSE fever if you know you're not going to stick around."

I look at Miss Shaw a bit desperately. "What do you think I should do?"

She smiles kindly. "Just decide, Emily. Honestly, I'm sure you'll be fine whatever you decide to do. Just **make** your **mind up** where you really want to be." I'm on my own with this.

The strange thing is that, even though this is one of the biggest decisions I've ever had to make, I do it more or less **immediately**. I want to stay here in London. You've heard all this before, I know. Last time I decided to stay here it was for Sam, though I tried to **deny** it. But this time I'm staying for ME. That's right, ME – the most important person in the world.

Being bilingual means there are always two MEs. And it looks like English ME has won – again! She's good! – against German ME. This time it's for all the right rea-

+++ vice versa – umgekehrt +++ to get all caught up in – von etw. komplett erfasst werden +++ to make one's mind up – sich entscheiden +++ immediately – sofort +++ to deny – leugnen +++

sons. I want to be in one education system. I have the feeling Chalk Farm School can offer me a little bit more than Hermann-Hesse-Gymnasium back home (never ever tell Betti and Merle that, never ever ever.) After all, it has a great hockey **pitch**. That was a joke, *klar*?

And yes, OK, there's a *tiny* part of me that knows how happy me staying here would have made the Queen Mother. I do feel like I **owe** her that. I like to think that she's looking down on me from some enormous **fluffy** cloud: *There, Queen Mum! That's her! That's Emily! The third generation of her family at the finest school in England! I had something so important to tell her.*

I make my decision to stay in London official: I tell Mum and Dad. I phone them, that very same day, and they're not surprised, I don't think, though Mum does sound a little bit sad.

"You're totally sure?" she says. I can hear Dad in the background: *She's staying on?* "Yes," I reply, **confidently**. I am. Mum sighs a really, truly, deeply heavy sigh. She'll let the school and Grandma's lawyer know.

I e-mail Betti and Merle to break the news to them as well. I don't think they'll be exactly shocked either. I think they've forgotten that I even lived in Berlin, sometimes, and, **occasionally**, I have to remind myself, too.

So now it's truly official, I'm staying here. No obsessions with boys. It's *work work work* time.

+++ pitch – Feld +++ to owe s.b. s.th. – jmdm. etw. schulden +++ fluffy – flauschig +++ confident – zuversichtlich +++ occasionally – gelegentlich +++

The Love Guru

Let's face it, though a life totally without boys might be much easier, it would also be unbelievably boring. Luckily, there is enough **intrigue** in other peoples' love lives to keep things at Chalk Farm just a little bit **spicy**.

It's unbelievable at the moment, in London. Honestly, if you're single – get yourself over here! Everyone I know is completely loved-up. It's like the **Pied Piper of Hamelin strolled** through the grounds of Chalk Farm School, playing *Love Is in the Air* and everyone followed him. It also seems like the Pied Piper also handed out flyers which said: *Talk to Emily! She's a love guru!*

What with the Ed affair and all the Sam drama, it seems I have the reputation of being a relationship veteran. This is a bit ironic since before I came to London I had zero interest from boys but still, it's fun. I'm asked so often for advice on other peoples' affairs/**crushes** that I'm thinking about setting up my own **practice**. I could have a **booth**, like the ones priests take confession in. I could set it up in the playground during breaks. Charge a small fee.

+++ intrigue – Faszination +++ spicy – *hier:* pikant +++ Pied Piper of Hamlin – Rattenfänger von Hameln +++ to stroll – spazieren +++ crush – Liebelei +++ practice – Praxis +++ booth – Kabine +++

Becks and Melissa ask me for some advice on the boys they fancy – a rugby boy and a **show-jumper**, apparently. I say vague things like: *Be yourself. Relax. Don't be too late for dates, but don't be too early. Don't talk in a stupid German accent.* They look at me like I'm a relationship genius.

It's all a laugh, hearing everyone's stories of romance. But, rather more seriously, I'm actually wishing that someone else would pay me a professional visit. There is one girl I know who might genuinely be in need of a bit of advice. And whom I have a horrible feeling won't take it.

Maudie. Yes, Maudie, my cool, funny best friend here. Maudie is dating Matt the bass player of the Kitty Gagarins and she is, it's safe to say, very, very **into** him. Just a bit *tooo* into him, actually.

I didn't really notice at first. I mean, Maudie *always* did talk about Matt a lot but, well, who doesn't when they first start going out with someone? And she did *always* seem to be texting or tweeting with him but again, show me a teenage girl who isn't **surgically** attached to her mobile phone or her computer. Our generation was born digital, right? And we fall in love digitally, too.

I suppose I was surprised that Maudie's obsession with Matt seemed to get worse as their relationship went on. She seemed to be texting him more often, not less, for instance. And I can tell you the *exact* moment that I *knew*

+++ show-jumper – Springreiter +++ to be into s.b./s.th. – jmdn./etw. mögen +++ surgical – chirurgisch +++

Maudie was too **addicted to** love: it was last Wednesday. OK, I don't know the exact time but sort of 12ish.

Maudie, Kim and me had met for lunch. The food at Chalk Farm is so terrible and we'd decided to "eat out": **scoff** kebabs in front of the school gates. Miss Bardwell hates us eating in the streets – it's unladylike, she **claims** – so I always take great pleasure in letting bits of meat and sauce fall over my uniform.

On the way to the kebab shop, I tell the girls about how it went at *The Sentinel*. Everything: the *amazing design of the offices* and *how much I learned*, blah, blah. Once I start talking about it, actually, I can't stop. I tell Maudie and Kim all about Chris, too: how rude and how strange he was at first, how seriously he seemed to take himself. And how weirdly hairy he was.

Maudie smiles. "Yeah, I know the type. He **has a chip on his shoulder**, right? They're always the same: you know, everyone else has it easy, they're the only ones that ever had to fight for everything. I hope you told him that you're not posh! You can't help it if your aunt's really good at her job, can you? Just ignore … whatshisname again?" she giggles. "Hairy boy. Jack Wolfskin."

Jack Wolfskin! Maudie's good. That is a funny name for Chris, actually. She's right, I shouldn't let him bother me so much. I suppose it's because I do feel guilty: I am always being given chances not because of what I can do, but because of who I am.

+++ to be addicted to s.b./s.th.– von jmdm./etw. abhängig sein +++ scoff – hastig gegessen +++ to claim – behaupten +++ to have a chip on one's shoulder – einen Minderwertigkeitskomplex haben +++

"Right," I mutter. By this time, we've got our kebabs and we're eating them, right in front of the school gates and in full view of the *Überwachungskameras* outside the Chalk Farm school gates. CCTV cameras they call them here. You can't move a centimetre in Britain without someone filming you. It's a weird feeling sometimes. Anyway, I make a stupid joke like: *Miss Bardwell will be watching the tapes of us eating our kebabs!* Something like that. Maudie and Kim laugh. **Encouraged**, I make a second joke about Maudie trying to get the tapes from the cameras so she could watch Matt leaving and entering St Dougan's.

Maudie didn't laugh, not because she was offended. No, she didn't laugh because *she was seriously thinking about my idea.* I swear, you could see the thought running through her head: *The tapes! Brilliant! I wonder where you get them? Then I would really know if he went to get chips at 5.17pm or not.* Yes, dear readers, it was at that moment that I knew Maudie had crossed the line. The fine line that exists between being *into* your boyfriend and being *obsessed* with him.

There are a couple of things that dragged Maudie across that line, I know. One is obvious: Maudie really, really likes Matt. He's exactly her type; he's cool, he's musical, he's funny. He's **smart**. He's a **straight down the line** kind of guy. It's all good.

The other thing that has made Maudie so super-**clingy** is not good. It's her bad experiences with boys before

+++ encouraged – ermutigt +++ smart – intelligent +++ straight down the line – durch und durch ehrlich +++ clingy – klammernd +++

Matt – firstly, with Ed Stanton, of course. Ed was definitely horrible to all three of us – Kim, Maudie and myself. For some reason, though, he was especially nasty to Maudie. The comments about her on his blog seemed, I don't know, just a little bit more "personal". Ed gave Maudie a really bad kissing **score**, for instance – my blood **boils** just thinking of it. That's why Maudie's also a bit paranoid about breath mints and things.

Then there was Rob, another disaster, the boy Maudie was interested in last term. He seemed to like Maudie, but went off with Cyclops instead, which also was a **blow** to Maudie's ego. That would be a blow to anyone's ego, of course. The only good thing is that Maudie is so busy watching Matt, she now seems to spend less time **monitoring** Cyclops, which was also a bit too much for a while.

It's perfectly logical – boys acting crazy with her has made *Maudie herself* crazy. I think she desperately wants to trust Matt, but experience tells her she just can't. And she's decided the answer is never to let Matt out of her sight. It's tragic.

I never said anything to Maudie, of course, apart from the CCTV joke. It didn't seem like any of my business. And I suppose I also thought that Matt was probably fine with having a girlfriend who always wanted to be with him. I don't really know Matt. I don't go with them on dates much, strangely enough.

But then … then I went "**anniversary** bowling" with them.

+++ score – Bewertung +++ to boil – kochen +++ blow – *hier:* Schlag +++ to monitor – überwachen +++ anniversary – Jubiläum +++

It's unusual, isn't it? Going bowling with your friends to celebrate the "three month anniversary" of your relationship? But that's what we do, just the five of us – Maudie and Matt, "the anniversary couple", Kim and her boyfriend Jonathan, plus Emily "**Gooseberry**" Hausmann.

The "anniversary" theme for the evening is Maudie's idea, naturally: she sends us all an e-mail – with a huge picture of her and Matt attached – to "celebrate with Matt and me" at a really **cheesy** and **rundown bowling alley** in Camden, popular in an "ironic" way with the rich kids at the boys' and girls' schools.

It must be one of those "couple jokes", I decide. It's quickly clear that only one half of the couple finds the joke funny. Even as we book our **lane**, I hear Matt muttering to Jonathan. "It's just a night out bowling, OK? It's not a celebration. Stupid idea."

Even hearing that doesn't ring alarm bells, not really. I'm too busy enjoying myself to really worry. I'm not bad at bowling – I used to go to a place at Alexanderplatz with Merle quite often (Betti absolutely does *not* "do" bowling). I'm in a good mood and doing well. I'm not only enjoying the opportunity to bowl, it's also really interesting to watch Maudie and Kim with their boyfriends. And it's only now that I notice how different they are with them.

Let's take Kim, first. She and Jonathan are a textbook couple. I mean, you could probably tell that she and

+++ gooseberry – Stachelbeere +++ cheesy – schäbig +++ rundown – heruntergekommen +++ bowling alley – Bowlingbahn +++ lane – Bahn +++

Jonathan were together if you didn't know them but only if you looked really carefully. Kim plays it cool. She spends a lot of time talking to me, she's concentrated on her game, bowling well. She certainly doesn't ignore Jonathan – and there's one moment where she whispers something in his ear and they look so **intimate** that I actually do miss having a boyfriend for the first time **in ages**.

So, Kim – 10 out of 10. Then, well, then there's Maudie. Her behaviour is more or less the opposite of Kim's. Maudie's far too busy either watching Matt or trying to kiss him to concentrate on bowling. Nearly all of her balls

+++ intimate – vertraut +++ in ages – seit ewigen Zeiten +++

end up in the **trough** at the side. She doesn't even seem to care. All she does seem to care about is sticking as close to Matt as she can. She follows him when he goes up to bowl, standing right behind him. She follows him when he goes to get the drinks, stuck to his back again. Matt, I see, has a really long face.

I only try and talk to Matt once to ask him how the Kitty Gagarins are getting on. He tells me what I already know; they've got a new drummer called Ian who's pretty good. They're working, slowly, on some new material …

But that's all the information I get because suddenly Maudie comes over and stands between us. "WHAT ARE YOU TWO WHISPERING ABOUT?" she shouts. It's a bit embarrassing.

It suddenly really hits me like a bowling ball in the face: it's creepy. Maudie's too clingy and it's obvious Matt is irritated by it, too. *Me and my shadow,* I hear him mutter again **at one point**, as Maudie nearly follows him to the *men's toilet.*

+++ trough – *hier:* Rinne +++ at one point – an einer Stelle +++

The End of the Affair

A conversation I have with Sam not long after the anniversary bowling disaster **confirms** it. I've been meaning to ask him about Matt for ages. So I call Sam from a **gazebo** in the gardens of Chalk Farm. It's a lovely spot and there's no one really around. I always used to ring him from one of the phone boxes in the school corridor but – hey! Now that I'm a **bona fide** rich girl I can **splash out on** mobile phone calls! Yippee!

We talk for about 45 minutes about life at opposite ends of the country before we finally get round to discussing Maudie and Matt. I just ask straight out, "What has Matt said about Maudie?"

It's not easy information to get – Sam is loyal – but in the end, I manage: "Matt likes Maudie, no question. But he says she's a bit **full on**. You know, **possessive**." Sam pauses. "Anyway, perhaps you could get her to **back off** a little? Matt likes his personal space. I don't know if Maudie realises that. Maybe you could mention it to her?"

+++ to confirm – bestätigen +++ gazebo – Gartenlaube +++ bona fide – echt +++ to splash out on s.th. – Geld für etw. hinauswerfen +++ full on – schonungslos +++ possessive – besitzergreifend +++ to back off – sich zurückziehen +++

Yikes. How on earth can I do that? Maudie will freak if I **hint** that she's too "possessive". I don't **have a clue** how to "mention" it to her. I'm still busy thinking about that when something else is mentioned. Something that should have been mentioned a while ago. Sam says quietly, "Look, there's something I've been meaning to ask you …"

I know it, in my heart. The moment has come: the end of the affair. I take a deep breath and say, "Go on."

Sam sighs. "Listen, I don't really have to say it, do I? You and me – it just can't work. I hope we'll always **stay in touch** but we, well, what I mean is: you're free to see other boys."

I don't **respond.** It's a lovely way to break up with someone, isn't it? *You're free.* Then Sam says, almost hopefully, "Anyone you've got your **beady** German eye on?"

I laugh. "No!" I shout. It's clear what this is about. "And you … anyone you've got your beady **Jock** four eyes on?"

Sam laughs. Sam coughs and then Sam finally gets it out: "Well, actually, now you ask: I was just wondering how you would feel if …"

If he went out with someone else, of course. How would I feel? Honestly, I'd feel like someone wearing high heels had stamped on my heart, probably. But it had to happen.

Sam talks quickly. He isn't dating anyone else, not yet. But he's thinking about it. He wanted to talk to me first.

+++ to hint – andeuten +++ to have a clue – Ahnung haben +++ to stay in touch – in Verbindung bleiben +++ to respond – antworten +++ beady – wach +++ Jock – Schotte/Schottin +++

"It's all a bit of a surprise," he mumbles. "I've known her for years. She asked me out a couple of weeks ago. It's funny: I suddenly realised I'd quite like to go out with her. Rona, her name is."

I interrupt him. "Sam," I say with as much **sincerity** as I can, "it's fine. Honestly, it's *fine*."

And then we change the subject and we chat some more. The conversation is so nice, somehow, that I almost forget that I *just split up officially with Sam.*

I sit in the gazebo for a while after my phone call – and my relationship – is over. It's nearly nine o' clock and I'm not allowed to be out much later. Still, it's a bright November night, cold and clear. I stare up at the stars, **struggling** to remember what my father taught me about *Sternbilder.* And I think over and over again: *Sam is going to go out with someone else.* I'm trying to get used to the idea of that. Of Sam holding someone else's hand. Him telling them that joke about the one-armed drummer from Liverpool. Him drumming his fingers nervously and then, just maybe, kissing her. Rona.

I think about this very hard for about 15 minutes. I remember that my father told me once: stars don't really die, they just burn out. That's how it feels with Sam and me. We didn't die, we just burned out. Better to burn out than to **fade away**, as Maudie's giant Kurt Cobain poster might have said.

Time's up. I've done it: I've felt very sorry for myself and very sad and now, I'm going to just concentrate on

+++ sincerity – Aufrichtigkeit +++ to struggle – sich bemühen +++ to fade away – verblassen +++

being happy for Sam. Enjoying my freedom. Using it. And trying to work out how I can help to save Maudie from relationship Armageddon.

I wonder briefly whether I should try to get Kim to say something to Maudie, then realise that would be the **coward**'s way out. I heard first-hand that Matt has a problem with Maudie being so possessive. It's **up to** me to try and let her know that in as tactful a way as possible.

I feel just a bit angry with Matt as I make my **reluctant** trip over to Bloomsbury the following evening, to pay a "surprise" visit to Maudie's dorm that evening. Why can't he just talk to Maudie? Tell her to back off himself? Why are all boys such emotional **cripples**?

Maudie's on the phone with her brother when I go into her dorm. It's her brother's birthday, I remember now. Maudie whispers, "Can you wait a sec?" And I sit on her roommate's bed – **thank goodness** she's not here – and then my heart nearly stops at what's happened to Maudie's room.

Last time I was here, which was a while ago I realise, most of Maudie's share of the wall space was taken up with her favourite huge poster of Kurt Cobain, who has always been her hero. But now, it seems, she's got a new idol. Now what I'm looking at is no longer a wall, it's a Matt Webb tribute installation. It's a ***shrine***.

Every millimetre of space in Maudie's part of the dorm

+++ coward – Feigling +++ to be up to s.b. – jmds. Sache sein +++ reluctant – widerwillig +++ cripple – Krüppel +++ thank goodness – Gott sei Dank +++ shrine – Altar +++

– apart from the one metre or so that Kurt has, by some miracle, hung onto – is covered with pictures of Matt. Matt alone, Matt with the band, Matt with Maudie, Matt with Sam, even. There aren't just pictures on the wall, there are framed photos next to Maudie's bed. There are photos stuck to her locker. I'm certain there will be a photo on the toilet if I look. Oh God. It's a stalker's paradise.

Maudie's now finishing her conversation with her brother. He obviously got *Guitar Hero* for his birthday: she seems to be discussing some of the tracks on that. But finally, finally, Maudie finishes her conversation. "Hi," she says brightly. "I didn't expect to see you tonight. Anything wrong? Is it Sam?"

I need to **work up to** discussing Matt, obviously, and, well, I should let Maudie know that I have now definitely split up with Sam. So I tell her. And that's when the conversation starts to go very badly wrong.

Maudie is **sympathetic** at first when I tell her about Sam and me being over. It's quickly clear, though: our breaking up confirms Maudie's philosophy – you should never let your boyfriend out of your sight!

"**It's a shame** about you and Sam, of course, but well ..." Maudie looks **coy**. "Boys like you to be there for them." She sits up suddenly, like she's just woken up. "Actually" – she looks at her watch – "is this going to take long? Because Matt will be coming out of band practice in about seven minutes or so."

+++ to work up to s.th. – auf etw. zusteuern +++ sympathetic – mitfühlend +++ it's a shame – es ist schade +++ coy – geheimnistuerisch

AAAAAGH! Enough! "Sometimes," I say carefully, nodding towards Maudie's Matt mural. "Some boys like a bit of *breathing space*."

Maudie **sniffs.** "I just don't believe that. Boys like to be made to feel like kings!"

Kings? Maudie once told me she was a riot girl third wave feminist! Kings? Boys aren't our **glorious** leaders, they're supposed to be our equals!

Maudie might have gone mad but she's not stupid, she knows what I'm driving it. She **scowls at** me. "What's this all about anyway? Has Matt said something to Sam?"

"No!" I say, trying to sound totally shocked. "I just thought the other night that Matt …at bowling … *oh, this is killing me saying this* … seemed a bit tense. I mean, he couldn't even go to thc toilet by himself."

That's done it. Maudie's face is bright red and she's furious. Her *Vokuhila* is probably about to **burst** into flames. She gets to her feet. "So I'm not allowed to need the toilet at the same time as my boyfriend, is that it? I have to coordinate my toilet visits so that I don't go together with Matt? That's **mental**."

My head is for the **chop**. "And you'll pardon me if I don't want to take relationship advice from you, Emily."

Maudie goes on some more but I don't think I want to remember what she said. It wasn't very nice, **put it that way**.

+++ to sniff – die Nase rümpfen +++ glorious – ruhmvoll +++ to scowl at s.b. – jmdn. mürrisch ansehen +++ to burst – ausbrechen +++ mental – verrückt +++ to be for the chop – zum Abschuss freigegeben sein +++ put it that way – lass es mich so sagen +++

Time for a quick exit. I leave the dorm, with thousands of Matt's eyes following me. *Help me*, they seem to say. *Get me down from here.* I **shudder**. "See you around," Maudie calls after me, sarcastically.

See you around, **roughly** translated into girlfight-speak, means *I hope I don't see you for ages.* Oh well. Thank heavens I have something else to cry and stress out about – really **polishing** my photography portfolio, so that I won't be ashamed to show it to Todd at *The Sentinel* on Saturday. Todd asked me to bring it with me: "Nora's always talking about what a **natural** you are at photography! I would really like to see if talent is genetic!" I panicked totally when he asked me, of course, but said yes. What else could I say?

I've now completely filled up the photo album that Nora gave me when I first arrived here in London. I've also nearly filled up the second portfolio. It's mainly full of pictures that I took of Camden street life a while ago but I've also added a few ones I've taken with my new camera. I'm *sort of* pleased with it.

But when Saturday rolls around and it's time to show my portfolio to Todd I'm even more nervous than I was on my first day. Nora won't be there either – she's **out and about** on **assignment** just outside London. In a way, I'm sort of relieved. It is my big chance to prove myself; to show *certain people* that I'm not just someone's niece.

+++ to shudder – erschaudern +++ roughly – grob +++ to polish – aufpolieren +++ natural – *hier:* Naturtalent +++ to be out and about – unterwegs sein +++ assignment – Auftrag +++

Now, walking with my portfolio in my hands towards Todd's office, I know that my biggest dream is being **put to the test**. It's the question that keeps me awake at night. Have I got talent? If not, can I get it somewhere? (Can you buy it online maybe?) And if I haven't got any, what do I *do* with the rest of my life?

As I carry on walking through the newsroom towards Todd's office, I can already see him talking to someone through the glass wall. Nightmare – it's *certain people.* Jack Wolfskin. What does he want? Shouldn't he be talking to unemployed **miners** or something? He doesn't care about art, about pretty pictures, beautiful things. He likes ugly reality.

Todd **greets** me warmly when I walk in. He turns to Jack Wolfskin and says, "You two know each other?"

Jack Wolfskin nods. He's sitting in front of one of the computers in Todd's office and he doesn't look up. Again. I tell you: this guy's charm school must have been bombed in the war. Then Todd says, "There's not much happening in the world today, apparently. I see you brought your portfolio" – he nods towards it, **tucked** under my arm – "so we've got plenty of time to look at it! Then I can show you a few computer tricks. Chris is also going to join us. He didn't have much else to do today either."

This is totally embarrassing. Now I have to get my pic-

+++ to be put to the test – auf die Probe gestellt werden +++ as – während +++ miner – Minenarbeiter/in +++ to greet – begrüßen +++ to tuck – stecken +++

tures out in front of Chris. Oh, he'll laugh! He'll do that horrible snorting noise again!

I pass my portfolio – my **soul**, really – over to Todd. He thanks me and starts to look through it. Jack Wolfskin continues to stare at his monitor, of course. But, after a while, I notice, he can't help himself. He looks over at my album, **casually** at first. Then, finally, he moves his chair and sits next to Todd and they go through it together.

Todd turns the pages slowly, asking questions and, it must be said, paying compliments. When he finally reaches the end, he **snaps it shut** and grins at me. "Well, photography really is in your blood, isn't it? Your aunt wasn't **exaggerating**. You are really talented. These are excellent, Emily!"

And even Jack Wolfskin **growls**, "They're good."

That was my fantasy feedback, of course, but you would not think so from what I do next. What I do next is excuse myself very quickly from Todd's office, go to the toilet and *cry my eyes out*. I can't help it, I'm **overwhelmed**. People have been nice about my photos before but those people were always 1) my family, 2) my friends, or 3) my teachers (so paid to be nice to me). I've never really had any objective feedback before.

And now, I've **impressed** the art director of one of Britain's biggest newspapers. Even more surprisingly, I impressed Jack Wolfskin.

+++ soul – Seele +++ casually – beiläufig +++ to snap s.th. shut – etw. zuklappen +++ to exaggerate – übertreiben +++ to growl – brummen +++ overwhelmed – überwältigt +++ to impress – beeindrucken +++

It's all too much, too good to be true. I suspect that somehow, this, the crying, is also **connected** to losing the Queen Mother and Sam. In a weird, complicated, possibly psychotic sort of a way.

I cry for more than 15 minutes. When I finally open my door, a quick look in the mirror confirms it: both my eyes are now three times the size of Cyclops' dodgy one. I'm very red, too. I have nothing with me, I realise: not a bit of make-up. I'd kill for a bit of **powder** or a **foundation stick** now. Oh well, there's nothing for it. I'll just **slink** behind my desk and try and work at the computer, with my head down. If anyone asks, I'll just say it's **hay fever** … oh **darn it**, it's nearly winter. I'll just say I'm allergic to … compliments.

But when I finally come out of the toilets, surprise, surprise, Jack Wolfskin is waiting for me.

He doesn't waste any time. "Come on," he says in a calm voice, **scratching** his head. "Todd ordered me to take you for a cappuccino."

And Jack Wolfskin actually *grabs me by the arm* and **leads** me to the lift. He doesn't say anything else to me, he doesn't even look at me. I should be angry but there's something so kind about his face – what you can actually see of it, under the beard – that I can't protest.

We don't say anything going up in the lift to the can-

+++ connected – verbunden +++ powder – Puder +++ foundation stick – Grundierungsstift +++ to slink – schleichen +++ hay fever – Heuschnupfen +++ darn it – verflixt +++ to scratch – kratzen +++ to lead – führen +++

teen either. We don't even say very much when we get our drinks. Then, as we're looking around for somewhere to sit, Jack Wolfskin says. "Want to sit out on the terrace today? It's actually quite mild."

Only someone who a) is British, and b) has as much body hair as old Mr Wolfskin here could possibly describe today's weather as "mild". A normal, non-hairy German would say it was: *eiskalt.* I still say yes, a bit **numbly**. I have a **cardigan** on and I do feel like some fresh air. Plus, there's a wicked view out over London from the canteen terrace. That should **cheer me up**.

Jack slides opens the door to the terrace; everyone inside the canteen stares and **shivers**. It seems even the British do think we're mad to sit outside at this time of year. "You're not even allowed to smoke here, so we really will be alone," grins Jack … Oh, enough already! He's being nice! Let's call him Chris again.

We sit on freezing cold, **damp** plastic seats – Chris gives them a quick **wipe** with his face! Joke! – and then we stare out at the city skyline. Neither of us says anything. Chris, I'm realising, just can't do "chat" and I don't feel like saying anything stupid, for a change. I just breathe in the clear London air – well, the **filthy** London air really. Still, it feels nice.

Finally, Chris says in a quiet voice, "Todd told me your grandmother died a few weeks ago?"

I look at him in surprise. I shouldn't be surprised, of

+++ numbly – benommen +++ cardigan – Strickjacke +++ to cheer s.b. up – jmdn. aufheitern +++ to shiver – zittern +++ damp – feucht +++ to wipe – wischen +++ filthy – dreckig +++

course. Nora's a living legend here at *The Sentinel* and they will all know that she lost her mother. You wouldn't have to be Stephen Hawking to work out that Nora's mother = my grandmother.

"She was quite a character, I hear." Chris takes a long **sip** of coffee and I nod. I can feel a **lump** in my **throat**. Terrific. I really don't want to start crying again.

There's another awkward silence before Chris says, "Do you like Helen Levitt?"

I gasp. *Do I like Helen Levitt??* Helen Levitt was one of the greatest streetlife photographers who ever lived. Helen Levitt was a ***goddess***. She took some awesome pic-

+++ sip – Schluck +++ lump – *hier:* Kloß +++ throat – Hals +++ goddess – Göttin +++

tures in New York. I like her in the same way that you "like" **oxygen** or being able to walk.

I've never actually met anyone else, though – except Nora, obviously – who's heard of her. I look at Chris, amazed. "Yes, I love her."

Chris nods. "I can see that in your photographs. She's clearly an inspiration."

I really must be dreaming all this. I've just had about the highest compliment you could ever wish to hear, **from** just about **the least likely person**. Mentioning me in the same breath as Helen Levitt – it doesn't get much better than that, ladies. If the terrace collapses now, I'll go down to my death with a big smile on my face.

Chris begins to talk about Helen Levitt's work some more – *I love that one at Halloween* – and all I can do is nod, furiously. I don't really trust myself to speak at the moment. Instead, I look closely at Chris's skin. It's actually quite hard to tell what age he is under all that hair. Good trick, Chris! Maybe that's what I'll do when I start getting old and **wrinkly**: grow a beard! **Save on** all those expensive face creams!

+++ oxygen – Sauerstoff +++ from the least likely person – von wem man es am wenigsten erwartet +++ wrinkly – faltig +++ to save on s.th. – bei etw. sparen +++

Teenwolf

We're back inside the canteen again, thankfully. Chris' **fur** obviously kept him warm but I've lost nearly all of the feeling in most of my body parts. As well as growing a beard in old age, I think I'll stop shaving my legs, too. That will get me through the winter. No **tights**!

I walk with Chris back to the lift. He mutters that *he has to go to see the Editor about something so he'll get off at a different floor*. He does so. "I'll see you around," he says a bit **vaguely**, as the doors close. It seemed as if we'd quite **bonded** sitting out there on the terrace but suddenly I feel quite shut out again. Shame.

I make my way back to see Todd, who's lovely to me. "Are you feeling better?" he asks gently. "Nora told us about your grandmother, of course. I'm very sorry. I sent Chris to cheer you up."

Todd suddenly bursts out laughing. "Did it work? He's not very **jolly**, is he? He's an old man in a young man's body, that one. You'd never guess he was only 17, would you now?" Todd leans in close to me, whispering, "Come on, admit it. You thought he was much older, didn't you?"

+++ fur – Pelz +++ tights *(pl.)* – Strumpfhose +++ vague – vage +++ to bond – zusammenschweißen +++ jolly – lustig +++

I smile. I almost giggle. Chris is *seventeen?????* It can't be true. How embarrassing. And how weird. I've been acting like I was with one of my aunt's friends or something and he's actually … more or less my age. Wow.

I'm surprised, as you might have **gathered**. I'd **got** Chris all **wrong**, it seems. He was kind to me today, on the whole. There really is a heart **beneath** the hair.

I find myself telling Kim about the kindness of the Wolfman later, when I meet her for my very-quickly-arranged-emergency-crisis-**summit**-talks-on-what-to-do-about Maudie. I'm to walk with Kim to her evening dance class: it was the only time we could find free. Kim smiles when I tell her about Chris. "Jack Wolfskin's not so scary after all, then? But you're not interested in him, right?"

"*No!*" I shout. "*No!*" I repeat. "*No!*" I say again, just to be totally clear. "*No!*" I add, just **for good measure**. "He's … *no*." It's all I can say. Chris is old enough to be my … **slightly** older brother, for goodness sake. Plus, any 17-year-old guy interested in a 15-year-old girl would have to be some kind of loser, right? And I don't think Chris is a loser. Intense, maybe, but not a loser. Plus, I'm off boys, remember?

"OK, take it easy!" laughs Kim. "It's just that when you talk about him …"

She doesn't finish her sentence and I don't want her to.

+++ to gather s.th. – *hier:* etw. verstehen +++ to get s.b. wrong – *hier:* ein falsches Bild von jmdm. haben +++ beneath – unter +++ summit – Gipfel +++ for good measure – sicherheitshalber +++ slightly – etwas

"I *respect* Chris," I say carefully. "He's smart and he knows what he wants. I suppose that's what I'd like …"

Kim nods. "Cool." She looks at her watch. "Listen, we'll have to hurry. I'm a bit late. What are we going to do about her then? Maudie? She's really annoyed with you but you're right, of course."

Kim sighs. "I tried to mention it to her before myself – the possessive thing – but she didn't want to know. She *is* pushing Matt away. It's written all over his face. I love Maudie but I'd **go nuts** if someone **crowded** me the way she's crowding him."

We look at each other. We both know what our options are. And our options are rubbish. We could 1) talk to Matt, 2) talk to Sam and get him to talk to Matt. And … that's about it. Or we could just wash our hands of it all and sit back and wait for Maudie to be dumped again. Nightmare. It took her ages to get over Ed. She'll become a **nun** if Matt drops her.

Kim sighs hard again and says, "Keep thinking about it. I've got to run. It's Tango time!" And she runs.

Keep thinking about it? I haven't done much else lately. It's hopeless. Maudie's relationship is **doomed**. Might as well just count the days and then be there to pick up the pieces. But until that terrible day … the prefect elections are **drawing** near.

Time is running out and I still have to talk to Sadie.

+++ to go nuts – verrückt werden +++ to crowd s.b. – jmdn. bedrängen +++ nun – Nonne +++ doomed – zum Scheitern verurteilt +++ to draw – *hier:* kommen +++

Amanda's election campaign got off to an impressive start last week. Believe it or not, she actually gave a Power Point presentation on why she should be made a prefect. It was unbelievable. Unbelievably horrible, that is. She brought her nasty pink laptop into Latin, while her stupid friend Laurie schlepped a video projector.

Amanda put on a really fancy, high-tech show, **I'll give her that.** She has some totally **jazzy** graphics. But stupidly, she makes her talk a "**SWOT**" **analysis.** I don't think she's absolutely clear what a SWOT analysis is because all she seems to talk about are her own **strengths**: leadership qualities, **compassion** – HA! HA!

It goes on and on. Amanda's apparent "organisational skills" are highlighted. Hmmm, strange, she was a real messy cow when I shared a dorm with her! She certainly couldn't organise her **pants** to go in the **laundry** bag, for instance.

It's all priceless, classic, **hilarious** stuff. Amanda concludes by making an emotional speech: "I know I have led a life of privilege. But I have known pain" – she points to her "bad" eye – "real pain. Social exclusion." She **glares** over **at** me. Me!

"So for all these reasons, I am certain I would make an excellent prefect. I would **relish** the challenge of being able to serve my classmates. Thank you. Any questions?"

+++ I'll give her that. – Das gestehe ich ihr zu. +++ jazzy – knallig +++ SWOT analysis – Analyse der Stärken, Schwächen, Chancen und Risiken +++ strength – Stärke +++ compassion – Mitgefühl +++ pants – Unterhose +++ laundry – Wäsche +++ hilarious – lustig +++ to glare at s.b. – jmdn. zornig anschauen +++ to relish doing s.th. – etw. sehr gern tun +++

My hand shoots up into the air. She's trying not to look at me … oh, I'll just shout it out then. "Amanda? SWOT actually stands for Strengths, **Weaknesses**, Opportunities and Threats. Could you tell us what your weaknesses are?"

Amanda glares at me, then remembers that this is, like, an *election* and you have to **pretend** to be *nice* to people if you want them to vote for you. She smiles a smile that would win Gold at the Annual **Fake** Smile Awards. "Well, I'm too emotional sometimes, like I said."

I nod enthusiastically: "Too emotional to do the job, is that what you're saying? You'd be crying all the time, is

+++ weakness – Schwäche +++ to pretend – so tun als ob +++ fake – falsch +++

that what you're saying?" Oh, I'm enjoying this. Miss Bardwell is looking like she'd like to drag me away.

"And what about your **threats**?" I say. It sounds a bit **ominous** again, the way I say it, I have to admit but that's good, eh? It's Amanda's stupid **fault** anyway – fancy doing a SWOT analysis of *yourself*! She's an **airhead**.

"Well," says Cyclops uncertainly. "Erm, I don't think …" She looks at Miss Bardwell.

There's nothing to say, of course. There are no threats because there are no other real candidates. That has to be changed!

I think quickly. Sadie's not here this morning; she's at the **opticians** getting her astigmatism looked at, she told us. She wouldn't **mind** if I suggested her name as another candidate, would she?

I do it: "Miss Bardwell," I say suddenly. "When will the other candidates get a chance to make presentations?"

Miss Bardwell looks **taken aback**. This is a one horse race so far and it's **plain** that she wants to keep it that way. But she recovers quickly. She even smiles. "Well, so far Amanda is the only one to have come forward to present herself. Everyone is welcome to do so. We do have limited class time, of course."

"Well, can Sadie do her candidate presentation on Monday?" I ask **boldly**. "She's standing for prefect and I'm her campaign manager," I add, lying.

+++ threat – Risiko +++ ominous – unheilvoll +++ fault – Fehler +++ airhead – Hohlkopf +++ optician – Optiker/in +++ to not mind s.th. – nichts gegen etw. haben +++ taken aback – verblüfft +++ plain – klar +++ bold – mutig +++

Amanda laughs. "Sadie Simple!" she **titters**. Then she sees that I'm serious and her face changes. She's cross. It's even worse for Miss Bardwell: she's trapped. She has no choice but to say *yes*, of course. Sadie will be allowed to give her presentation on Monday. Miss Bardwell smiles and winks at Cyclops. "I don't suppose the presentation will take very long." She clearly can't believe that Sadie will have anything to say.

The class is over and I feel triumphant. Terrified. I **made a stand against** Cyclops and Bardwell. Now I just have to let Sadie know that I've **volunteered** her to run as a prefect. **No big deal**.

Lots of other people think that it is. Melissa, for instance. She grabs me by the arm as we leave Latin: "Are you completely *crazy*? Sadie doesn't want to be a prefect! Why don't you stand yourself? You'd get more ..."

Melissa's about to say *more votes than Sadie* but she stops herself just in time. But I don't agree, for two reasons. Firstly, my "underdog" theory. Sadie's a good girl who needs a break. And, secondly, I really don't want to go up against Amanda again. I've spent enough of my life doing that.

To Melissa I say, "Being a prefect would **boost** Sadie's confidence!" Well, it would. I've had a dream for ages about finding some way to make Sadie believe more in herself. She's the kind of person who apologises if *you* stand on *her* toe.

+++ to titter – kichern +++ to make a stand against s.th. – sich gegen etw. auflehnen +++ to volunteer – sich freiwillig melden +++ no big deal – keine große Sache +++ to boost – verstärken +++

It's true that she doesn't have all that many friends but I think a lot of girls like her. I just can't believe that all these girls I see now walking past me in the corridor – nice, pretty, smart girls – want Amanda to be prefect. I can't. I have more **faith** in human nature than that!

Now I just have to convince Sadie …

I have to find her first. Even though I share a dorm with her, she never seems to spend much time there. I thought at first she might have a secret lover or something but I soon found out the truth: she plays a lot of Scrabble online. I try the computer rooms and sure enough, behind the third door I open, there she is.

Sadie's not very excited to see me, her campaign manager-**in-waiting**. "I'm in the middle of a game," she says **flatly**. "Is it important?"

She doesn't *quite* collapse with fear when I tell her what I did in Latin today. "You did *what*?" she says **faintly**. "Emily, I can't. I don't want to be a prefect."

"Oh, come on," I say impatiently. "Just think of all the **benefits**." I think quickly: *what are the benefits?* "The power. You can tell people what to do."

Sadie looks unimpressed. "I don't want to tell people what to do," she mutters. "I just want a quiet life."

It's time for my big speech. I've been preparing it for a while. And I give it all I've got. I talk to Sadie, believe it or not, about *die Weiße Rose*. Don't laugh. I tell her all about

+++ faith – *hier:* Glaube +++ in-waiting – *hier:* zukünftig +++ flat – *hier:* lahm +++ faint – matt, schwach +++ benefit – Vorteil +++

Sophie Scholl. Then I talk about Rosa Luxemburg. Rosa Parks. Women called Rosa who stood up for what they believed in. Against dictators and bus passengers. I think I even mention Winston Churchill standing up to Hitler. In the background, while I speak, trumpets play. Don't they? I can hear them anyway.

When I've finished, 25 minutes later – I can tell that I've got her. I've convinced her. Sadie looks inspired. And worried: "We've got to put together a Power Point presentation by Monday???"

Chinese Democracy

Luckily, Sadie actually knows how to work with Power Point. She'll do the technical stuff and I have to help her decide what to say and how to say it. We spend hours preparing it, working until just before lights out. The first time Sadie tries to speak is a disaster, but she actually gets much better. She's definitely getting into the idea, I can tell.

Then we **rehearse** it in front of Melissa and Becks after lights out. Yes, in the dark. I can't actually see Melissa or Becks' face – the lights are out, remember? – but I can tell they're impressed. Sadie's brilliant. Brilliant. We can get her elected, I know it.

We go through her presentation at least eight times on Sunday night. Sadie's done some excellent graphics and we've got a strong campaign. The other girls should vote for Sadie for loads of reasons: she's a **scholarship** girl, she's an underdog, she's not Amanda, Miss Bardwell doesn't like her. We have a strong **manifesto**.

On Monday morning, we are 90% ready. But there's no point in being even 100% ready, of course. When Sadie

+++ to rehearse – proben +++ scholarship – Stipendium +++ manifesto – Wahlprogramm +++

and me try to set our things up, Miss Bardwell says **briskly**, "I'm sorry, girls, but exams are coming. There's simply no time available for any further presentations. We must do more grammar practice ..."

I can't stop myself, I shout out, "But that's not fair! Sadie worked really hard on her presentation ..."

Miss Bardwell gives me her stoniest look. "I repeat: there is *no time*, Emily. Have I made myself clear?"

Oh, yes, definitely. There's no time. And there's definitely no freedom of speech here in Kensington, **none**. Right, well, Sadie's just going to have to have a guerrilla-style election campaign! A **viral** one. I gather together all the e-mail addresses of everyone in the class and I send round a group mail, asking them all to sign an online petition, protesting against how unfair the prefect elections have been. I'm really happy because loads of girls agree. I also try to get an idea of who will vote for Amanda: no one, it seems! I suppose there are a couple of girls too ashamed to tell me, but even so, Amanda has no chance.

I then invite everyone who "believes in democracy" to come over the Kensington **common room** on Thursday night to hear Sadie's presentation. About 20 girls **turn up** and Sadie does a brilliant job. We've even got badges to give them all as they leave: *Sadie Reece: The Democratic Candidate.*

Sadie will win. It should be a **landslide**. We should be

+++ brisk – energisch +++ none – keine/r +++ viral – *hier:* rasend schnell bekannt +++ common room – Gemeinschaftsraum +++ to turn up – erscheinen +++ landslide – überwältigender Sieg +++

driving round Chalk Farm school **drive** in an open-top bus, waving at our thousands of cheering supporters any time soon.

Then, the next day, I'm going to prepare some flyers when I see Melissa coming down the corridor towards me. She looks gloomy. "There's a notice hanging in the hall. I think you'd better come and see it."

The "notice" is, in fact, just a single piece of A4 paper with some words typed on it. The words say: *The results of the election for position of prefect in Kensington House are as follows: Amanda Dobson has been **duly** elected prefect.*

+++ drive – Auffahrt +++ duly – wie erwartet +++

That's it. That's all it says. No number of votes. No **percentages**. It just can't be possible!

It's Friday evening. Miss Bardwell must have hoped she could **slip it in** under the radar. Announce it when everyone's gone home for the weekend, so everyone will have forgotten about it by the time Monday morning rolls around. **Nice one**. No way.

I'm still in a **foul** mood when I arrive at *The Sentinel* the next day. I love being there but I can't quite get it out of my head. It's so unfair. It's nothing, of course – just a meaningless stupid job that Sadie didn't really want anyway. But it still hurts.

I don't see Jack Wolfskin – Chris! – that morning and I'm so busy with Todd showing me how to **photoshop** some images of an actress that morning that I don't have much time to think about him. When I go to get lunch, however, he's there again.

Chris actually waves one of his hairy arms at me to indicate that I should join him! I do and he doesn't even say hello, he just starts talking **straight away** about the demonstration in London which is today's big story. "I was out there interviewing some of the people taking part," he says, his eyes **glowing**. "I love it. Real front-line journalism, talking to people about what matters. People standing up for principles, what they believe in: democracy."

+++ percentage – Prozentsatz +++ to slip s.th. in – *hier:* etw. unterschieben +++ nice one – *hier:* netter Versuch +++ foul – schlecht +++ to photoshop – ein Bildbearbeitungsprogramm anwenden +++ straight away – sofort +++ to glow – glänzen +++

I look at Chris. Standing up for what you believe in, eh? Democracy, eh? But I can't bother Chris with something as unimportant as the prefect election. He's interested in people who have lost their jobs or their homes standing up for themselves. Not a **bunch of** posh girls fighting about nothing.

But, somehow, I do find myself telling Chris all about our repressive Chalk Farm regime. I think he'll hate me at first for being at a posh school but he seems fine with that. And, actually, he really cares! He's **indignant**! He snorts the way he did when I first met him! "Well, that's awful! Do the parents know that they're paying a fortune for their daughters to be taught that **cheating** wins?"

Wow. Chris really is a born reporter and he can smell a good story. He grins. He's already finishing off his drink, closing his laptop. "Emily, shall I come and **cover** the story? I probably can't do it officially for the newspaper or anything but I could do it for my blog."

Chris actually smiles at me. He's totally into this rebellion. "Have you thought about organising some immediate action? You know – a strike at the school?"

I gasp. A strike? "That would be …" I can't find the right word at first. Then I do – the right word is *fantastic.*

"I hope you're not **leading** my niece **astray**, Chris!" says a voice behind my head suddenly. Nora! My heart does a

+++ a bunch of – ein Haufen +++ indignant – aufgebracht +++ to cheat – betrügen +++ to cover s.th. – *hier:* über etw. berichten +++ to lead s.b. astray – jmdn. auf Abwege bringen +++

little dance, as it always does when it – and the rest of my body – sees her. She's just back from her assignment and is starving, she tells us, sitting down next to Chris and me, a plate of pasta in her hand. She has no idea what we're discussing, of course. When we tell her, her face falls. She goes quite pale. Miss Bardwell's magic touch.

"Oh Emily," she says slowly. "Are you sure it's worth **antagonising** Miss Bardwell? She can be amazingly cruel. Perhaps …" She **catches Chris's eye**. He's giving Nora a very **injured** stare. "Chris is right, too, of course," Nora says quickly. "One should stand up for what one believes in." She takes a mouthful of pasta. "Hmm," she says, looking thoughtful. "And you're really going to go with her on Monday, Chris? You're serious? Need a photographer?"

A strike at Chalk Farm School. It's mental. It's a **suicide** mission. It's the most exciting thing that has happened to me in ages. And, actually, I discover organising a strike is as easy as organising a **slumber party**. I simply send another group e-mail round the girls in my class – except Cyclops and Laurie, of course. Some of the answers I get back are a bit nervous but, in the end, everyone agrees that the election result is a slap in the face. Our class will strike in protest during our next Latin class. *Vive la Révolution!*

I really do feel a bit Che Guevara, actually, as I head down to Latin on Monday morning. Strike Day. My faith-

+++ to antagonise s.b. – sich jmdn. zum Feind machen +++ to catch s.b.'s eye – jmds. Blick auffangen +++ injured – verletzt +++ suicide – Selbstmord +++ slumber party – Party mit Übernachtung +++

ful **comrades in arms**, Melissa and Becks, are at my side. No one speaks. This is probably the most radical thing that's *ever* happened at Chalk Farm School.

Nora and Chris will come over later. They won't actually be allowed in the school building itself, of course, but we agreed that all the "strikers" would meet outside afterwards on the playground to pose for a photo shoot. The girls are all excited about this.

Everyone takes their seats; we're early. The only ones who aren't here yet are Cyclops and Laurie. Luckily, they're always slightly late because they know they can be. Miss Bardwell doesn't mind what they do.

I go to the front of the classroom and stand in front of the blackboard, glancing nervously towards the door. I say quickly, "All you have to do is not do anything: if Bardwell asks you to take out your books, none of you do it. And don't say anything to her. I'll explain what's happening …"

A worried looking girl with a **chestnut bob** called Belinda puts her hand up. "We won't be **expelled**, will we?"

"No," I say confidently. "That's why it's important that we all stand together: the school can't afford to expel us all. It can't. There's a financial crisis going on, in case you hadn't heard, and private schools are feeling it badly."

Suddenly the door opens and everyone **jumps**. Belinda even screams loudly. It's Cyclops and Laurie. Game on.

+++ comrade in arms – Waffenbruder +++ chestnut bob – kastanienbrauner Bubikopf +++ to expell – *hier:* von der Schule werfen +++ to jump – zusammenzucken +++

The Glasses of a Born Leader

"What are you up to, Hausmann?" Amanda says at once. "Don't forget I'm a prefect now, so I can take you to Mrs Randall straight away. Stealing from Miss Bardwell's desk, were you?"

I smile **grimly**. Amanda has just confirmed everything that we were afraid of: she will abuse her power, as sure as eggs is eggs. She's already had her gold braid **stitched** on to her blazer and is wearing her prefect badge.

I go over to my seat, with Amanda eyeing me suspiciously. She can **sense** something is going on but has no idea what, I'm sure of it. It seems that everyone in class has kept their mouths shut. My girls!

Amanda and Laurie are also taking their seats by the time Miss Bardwell enters the room. She's hurrying as she's almost late, which is unusual. I catch Sadie's eye: she winks. She got new glasses at the opticians last week and they really suit her. She looks good. Those are the glasses of a natural born leader.

Miss Bardwell barely glances at us. She's busy getting her textbook out. "Right, girls," she mutters, "let's not

+++ grim – grimmig +++ to stitch – nähen +++ to sense – spüren +++

waste time. We were on page 48 and you had exercise 4 as homework. Let's go through that."

Honestly? It actually feels really *strange* not to do what Miss Bardwell says. It's automatic to **obey**, we're all like well-trained **Alsatians**. Still, we manage. No one moves, except Cyclops and Laurie, who eagerly get their books out, **wagging their tails**.

It takes Miss Bardwell a few seconds to notice that anything's wrong. She's busy looking at the exercise herself and frowning. Then it **dawns on** her that only two girls actually have a copy of *Serve! Book 3, Intermediate* on their desks. She finally looks up, astonished and says angrily: "Girls? Are you **deaf**? Page 48, immediately!"

Again no one moves. It's like musical statues, without the music. And if there *were* music playing here right now, it'd be that kind of old spooky soundtrack.

Miss Bardwell places her hands on her hips and says loudly, "Is this some kind of a joke? If it is, it is extremely unfunny. Anyone who wishes to receive a good grade at the end of term should open their books at once!"

I see Melissa hesitate. Meilssa always gets good grades, of course, and she's plainly horrified by the idea of getting a bad one. Her arm moves just ever so slightly in the direction of her school bag. Then she gives her long hair a shake, the way that horses do. Perhaps she's thinking of them right now. Perhaps she's thinking: *If we tolerate this, then our horses will be next.*

+++ to obey – gehorchen +++ Alsatian – Schäferhund +++ to wag one's tail – mit dem Schwanz wackeln +++ to dawn on s.b. – jmdm. klar werden +++ deaf – taub +++

I know it's time to speak. I've rehearsed what I have to say many times but suddenly it's hard to get the words out. Then I see that Miss Bardwell's hand, the one holding her book, is shaking. She's really scared, I realise.

And that gives me a kick I need. I get to my feet and say, in what I hope is a clear, calm voice, "We won't be taking part in today's lesson, in protest against the unfairness of the recent prefect election."

"You … *stupid cow!* Who on earth do you think you are? How dare you …"

Cyclops, of course, furious. Miss Bardwell says **tetchily**, "Quiet, Amanda." She hasn't taken her eyes off me. I must not look away. I force myself to continue meeting her eye but I take my seat again. I fold my arms across my chest.

Miss Bardwell finally stops trying to make a hole in my face with her eyes. She looks around the room, smiling icily. "So, we're striking, are we? How very *rebellious.* How very *stupid.*" She hisses the last word. "Any girl who does not open her book within the next minute will face serious disciplinary action. I'm sure no one wants to **threaten** their future."

Even though we'd agreed to stay silent, Sadie can't hold back. She suddenly shouts out, "We simply wanted a fair election, Miss! It's not possible that so many people voted for Amanda. You're supposed to be a role model and you cheated!"

Sadie – the mouse that roared. I couldn't be prouder if I were her mother.

+++ tetchy – gereizt +++ to threaten – *hier:* gefährden +++

Miss Bardwell is trying not to completely **lose her temper**, I can tell, but she's close, very close … oh no. Shame. She's **composed herself**. She says simply, closing her textbook. "Very well, girls. I can see my presence is pointless. Anyone who wishes may now join me in my office for a tutorial."

Amanda and Laurie leap to their feet, as do, disappointingly, two other girls, Belinda and Marcia. Oh well. No one else moves, though. *United we stand*, more or less.

"Very well," says Miss Bardwell. *Very well.* She smiles grimly and leaves, followed by the four *Streikbrecher.* The mother of all **rows** will follow.

As soon as they've left the room, a small cheer goes up. It's not yet clear that we have anything to celebrate but at least we didn't **back down**. We made our point. This is better than *1. Mai in Kreuzberg*!

Then I realise everyone is looking at me, waiting for a signal. And I think suddenly: *No point in sitting here waiting for the hammer to fall.* I'm pretty sure Nora and Chris will already be outside.

I am just about to say something when I realise that this is Sadie's show. Sadie's the boss. I nod in her direction. "Sadie?" I say. I'm **passing the torch**. And the boss picks it up and says brightly, "I think our photo opportunity is waiting for us, girls. Shall we go?"

+++ to lose one's temper – die Geduld verlieren +++ to compose oneself – sich beruhigen +++ row – Streit, Auseinandersetzung +++ to back down – nachgeben +++ to pass the torch (to s.b.) – (an jmdn.) übergeben +++

We troop outside behind Sadie, our unelected beloved leader. She's found her cause and found herself, it seems. We walk down the corridor towards the main door: no one stops us. There's no sign of Miss Bardwell. We simply walk out into the fresh Red November air. Sure enough, there are Nora and Chris, standing near the gates and smiling.

Yes, Jack Wolfskin – actually smiling. He comes over to me quickly and then **punches** me on the shoulder! "Well, how did it go?" Nora is listening, too, nodding encouragingly.

"We did it," I say, a bit nervously. "Or rather we did nothing, actually. Miss Bardwell walked in and told us to get our books out …"

"… and we didn't move a muscle!" **yells** Sadie suddenly. She's all **flushed** in the face and giggly. If I didn't know her better, I'd say she'd been at Mrs Randall's sherry. "It was *so* brilliant!"

Chris roars: "*Yessssss!*" Almost as if Sadie had scored a goal. He gives her a little hug, saying, "Come on, give me an interview." And he gets out his **dictaphone**. He's being *playful.* He's almost being flirtatious.

I may as well tell you here, in the interests of full **disclosure**, I feel a tiny bit jealous at this point. Just a tiny bit. Chris never seems to want to touch me – apart from a rather painful shoulder punch – and yet there he is, hugging Sadie and, oh great, Melissa, too, now. Anyone else?

+++ to punch – schlagen +++ to yell – schreien +++ flushed – rot +++ disclosure – Enthüllung +++ dictaphone – Diktafon, Diktiergerät +++

It's stupid, of course. It's not like I fancy Chris or anything ... no, really ... but he's cool and I would really like him to like me. So far, he doesn't seem to, not very much.

Anyway, Nora is now **barking** at the girls, like a talking sheepdog, trying to get them into the right formation. "OK, Sadie at the front. Becks, isn't it? You're at the back. And my beautiful **Bolshevik** niece, over here! In the middle! Centre stage!"

I line up in the middle of the front row, between Sadie and another girl, Angela. Nora starts to take photos. "Say Kimchi!" she grins. We smile a bit, someone shouts, *Viva the Chalk Farm Revolution!*

There are even some **passers-by** watching us, through the school fence. Old people mainly and one girl in a grey **trilby** hat and sunglasses. It's **odd** weather for sunglasses, I think absently. Even Cyclops has had hers amputated from her face.

I seem to catch the eye of the girl in sunglasses but I can't be sure, as I can't see her eyes. She moves off, walking down Chalk Farm Road quickly in the direction of the underground station. There's something about her walk that's familiar. It's Olga Petrova's walk, I'm sure of it.

Olga Petrova was my roommate and Melissa's ex-best friend. She was taken out of our school, last Christmas, shipped back to Florida to get married by her strict Russian father. She *can't* be in London! She'll be **trying on veils** in Florida, right now. I follow her with my eyes as

+++ to bark – anblaffen +++ Bolshevik – Bolschewik/in, Kommunist/in +++ passer-by – Passant/in +++ trilby – Filzhut +++ odd – merkwürdig +++ to try on – anprobieren +++ veil – Schleier

she **scurries off** down the street. It can't be her! I'm just about to say something when I hear Becks gasp. "Oh gawd, girls. She's coming over!"

No prizes for guessing. No, it's not Olga. I'm quite certain I'm the only one who noticed her. Becks is talking about Miss Bardwell, who's now running, actually running towards us. She's fast. I think Becks is quite impressed: "Not a bad technique," she mutters **approvingly**.

Cyclops and Laurie are **trailing** behind Miss Bardwell. I don't think they can keep up. Even though they are 20 years younger than her, Miss Bardwell is clearly driven by **fury** and **hatred**. If I were Nora, I would flee. And now.

+++ to scurry off – wegeilen +++ approving – zustimmend +++ to trail – trotten +++ fury – Wut +++ hatred – Hass +++

But Nora never runs away from things. Now that she's seen Miss Bardwell, she simply turns to face her. She doesn't move from the spot. Chris, of course, has never met Miss Bardwell before but he turns and mouths at me: *Is that her?* All I can do is nod. It's horrible.

Miss Bardwell has reached us now. She doesn't even glance at any of us girls, all still standing in our rows, totally silent. No, like a heat-seeking **missile**, she goes straight for Nora. Her eyes are wild, her hair is all over the place. She **lunges for** Nora's camera, screaming: "YOU! I should have guessed immediately that you were behind all this. Give me that!"

Nora looks **shaken** but she's calmly holding her camera away from Miss Bardwell. Instinctively, Chris **snatches** it from Nora, to keep it safe. Miss Bardwell gasps and turns on him. "How dare you? You are both **trespassing** on school property. You have no right to …"

Chris quickly **slings** Nora's camera over his shoulder and holds out his other hand to Miss Bardwell. "Chris Morris from *The Sentinel*," he says calmly. He's loving this. "We're here to cover the strike and the **allegations of fraud** …"

Miss Bardwell snorts. She doesn't shake Chris's hand, surprisingly. "I might have known! That silly left-wing **rag**!"

Chris pulls himself up to his full height, which is quite

+++ missile – Rakete +++ to lunge for – sich stürzen auf +++ shaken – erschüttert +++ to snatch – schnappen +++ to trespass – unerlaubt betreten +++ to sling – hängen +++ allegation – Behauptung +++ fraud – Betrug +++ rag – Schmierblatt +++

tall – he's an English Yeti! "Would you care to make a statement, Miss Bardwell? You've been accused of …"

"Never mind what I've been accused of! You should be reporting on her … this home **wrecker** here!" She **jabs** a bony finger in Nora's direction.

I'm next, of course. The bony finger is now aimed at me. "And you … you're nothing but trouble, Hausmann! Your grandmother would be turning in her grave! **I'll see** you are removed from this school …" Amanda, who's been strangely quiet till now, cheers.

I look up, for some reason. I don't like to think of Grandma being down there in the ground. She'll be cheering me on from her cloud, right now, with Mr Churchill at her side! Standing up for yourself in the face of evil is what made Britain great.

Chris rolls his eyes. He's not scared of Miss Bardwell at all. "Are you really saying that you would expel a pupil who simply wanted to report cheating …"

Miss Bardwell **interrupts** him, "*What I say is none of your business.* Now leave the school before I call the police! And I am perfectly serious: hand that camera over. It's illegal to take pictures of children under 16 without the **consent** of their parents."

When Miss Bardwell wants something, she's difficult to **refuse**. Even Chris is now looking a little bit uncertain. "The camera," she says again coldly. "If one word of this conversation appears, I will take great pleasure in burn-

+++ wrecker – Zerstörer/in +++ to jab – *hier:* strecken +++ I'll see – Ich werde dafür sorgen +++ to interrupt – unterbrechen +++ consent – Zustimmung +++ to refuse s.b. – jmdn. zurückweisen +++

ing down the building of your stupid, filthy paper, with its stupid photographer here still inside …"

And then Chris plays his joker. He raises one arm: it looks for a second as if he really will give Bardwell the camera. But, in fact, he isn't holding the camera in his raised arm: it's his Dictaphone. It's on and running. Everything that Miss Bardwell has said, every word, every hate-filled furious word, is on tape.

Chris smiles at Miss Bardwell. "Anything else you'd like to say? And please, feel free to call the police. I'm sure they'd love to hear what's on this tape …"

Game over. It must be. Chris and Nora are preparing to retreat. Miss Bardwell has lost, somehow. She can't stop them leaving with the dictaphone and the camera, of course. She has no choice but to watch them go.

It's Nora's good manners, ironically, that cause everything to fall apart. She could just go now, not look back, just go. But instead she says, "Connie? It doesn't have to be like this." She holds out her hand. It's a stupid thing to do, she'll admit it afterwards, but she has to try. She has class, Nora. She's civilised. And that's when it happens: Miss Bardwell completely **melts down** emotionally. Her right hand doesn't reach out to shake Nora's; instead, it reaches out and slaps her, hard, across the face.

The sound echoes across the whole school grounds; the sound, as I think even the most brain dead of my classmates realise, that marks the end of a teaching career.

+++ to melt down – *hier:* zusammenbrechen +++

Take Me Home

What happens next is all a bit of **a blur**. Chris and me grab a shaken Nora and head for the school gate. There's no way I'm going back into school. I mean, I'm **assuming** that my life at Chalk Farm is over anyway, inheritance or no inheritance.

I only glance back once and see my classmates trooping inside Chalk Farm School, my loyal girls, with their new leader Sadie. I can't see Miss Bardwell anywhere. I'd love to know what's happening but I'll be able to find out on Twitter in about 20 minutes, I suppose.

Nora's car is parked near the school; Chris will drive us to Nora's flat in Fitzrovia, Nora is too **wobbly** to walk. Her face is very red, I swear you can see a handprint.

Chris **takes charge** once we're inside the flat. He gets Nora an icepack for her face which still looks sore. Then he makes us all a cup of tea and even finds a packet of **digestive biscuits**, well hidden in one of Nora's cupboards. The three of us then sit in a row on Nora's sofa, all stunned, staring at the teapot and biscuits.

+++ to be a blur – verschwimmen +++ to assume – annehmen +++ wobbly – wackelig +++ to take charge (of) – sich kümmern (um) +++ digestive biscuit – Vollkornkeks +++

Chris finally says, “I don’t really know what to do with the story, to be honest, any ideas? I mean, it could all be a bit personally embarrassing for you, Nora. A scandal.”

Nora puts her hands over her ears. “Not now. I’m going to lie down, I’m totally **shattered**. Let me sleep for an hour, then I’ll decide what to do.” She disappears into her bedroom, closing the door quietly behind her.

That leaves Chris and me alone together, still sitting on the sofa, uneasily. I feel really **flat**, actually. I caused all these problems for Nora and I’ve just messed up my school career, all my plans. It feels like my whole life just went horribly wrong.

I would love a hug from someone right now. Unfortunately, I’m sitting next to the one person in the world that I can’t ask for one.

Chris says suddenly, “That was pretty heavy, wasn’t it? It’s not your fault, though. You did the right thing.” Then he puts his arm around me, just like that. “You know, I thought you were just some stupid **nepotist brat** at first. But you’ve really got spirit …”

I can’t help it, I melt. Having Chris’s arm around me feels absolutely amazing. I let my head fall on his shoulder. I expect him to pull away from me sharply but he doesn’t. Instead, he starts to **stroke** my hair. “You’ll be fine,” he mutters. I don’t feel fine. **My stomach is churning**, my **palms** feel cold and sweaty.

+++ shattered – fix und fertig +++ flat – platt +++ nepotist brat – Göre, die durch Vetternwirtschaft zu etwas kommt +++ to stroke – streicheln +++ my stomach is churning – mir dreht sich der Magen um +++ palm – Handfläche +++

It feels so nice in Chris's arms, so natural. Natural as it was with Sam. And it's almost, sort of, like, I *forget* that I'm not actually in Sam's arms. I *forget* that these are a completely different set of arms that absolutely do not belong to me. They might even belong to someone else, for instance. Chris might have a girlfriend for all I know.

But it feels like the world has gone insane. I've got nothing to lose now anyway, have I? I can't help it, I just want to be kissed. I haven't kissed anyone for weeks now, and I miss it so. So let me be very clear about this: I kissed Chris. *Punkt.* And let me be very clear about something else: Chris kissed me back.

The kiss goes on just a bit too long for it to be any kind

of accident. We kiss for what is probably about three minutes and – I'm sorry Sam and I'm not sorry Ed – is the best, most passionate kiss of my life. It feels odd at first, kissing someone with a beard, but the hair is much softer than you'd think and Chris is a great kisser. All I can think while it's happening is: I will pay for this but it will be worth it. When I'm old and lonely, I will be able to draw on the memory of this kiss and how exciting it was and I won't feel so old and lonely any more.

Finally, Chris pushes me away, ever so gently, and says, "Emily …"

I get to my feet. I know what he's going to say and I don't want to hear it. It's **ridiculous**, I know. I'm standing here in my school uniform, for goodness sake! It's like a scene from the Britney Spears *Hit Me Baby One More Time* video. Lolita!

I head for the front door. I just want to get away. Chris doesn't move from the sofa. He doesn't try and stop me leaving. He looks a bit like Nora did after she'd been slapped in the face, totally shocked.

I don't really know where I'm going. I **stagger** out of the door. I haven't got a penny on me. I **wander** the streets for a while, like the survivor of a nuclear attack. I'm **giddy**, totally giddy. My head is **spinning**. *What a morning.*

I can't help it: my feet are drawn back to school. I walk all the way. It's like I have giant magnets in my shoes. I

+++ ridiculous – lächerlich +++ to stagger – wanken +++ to wander – durchstreifen +++ giddy – schwindelig +++ to spin – *hier:* sich drehen

have to know what's happening. I started this whole thing, I made this whole mess. I have to go back and face the music. The song will probably be: ***Hit the Road, Jack!*** of course. But really, the idea of getting on a plane and going back to Berlin doesn't seem so bad right now.

I look at my watch. It's lunchtime, thankfully. I could slip into the cafeteria or I could just lie down on my bed for ten minutes. Oh, that sounds nice. I start to go up the stairs to our dorm and walk straight into Melissa and Becks coming down the stairs.

"Emily!" cries Melissa. "There you are," says Becks at the same time. "Oh, we were worried!"

"Not as worried as I was," I mutter. "Have we been expelled?" I suddenly remember that I wanted to ask Melissa about Olga: whether it's possible that I really saw her watching us from Chalk Farm Road this morning but I realise that will have to wait.

Melissa's frowning. "It's been really strange. We all just came back inside and waited in the hall for a bit. We were so sure someone would come but no one did! Then we just went to our next lesson. Not a word's been said yet. And no one's seen *Miss Bardwell*."

Becks giggles. "I mean, we're all just waiting to get our marching orders really. But now we've got English **Lit** and we're just going to go and see what Mr Benn says to us there."

+++ Hit the road, Jack! – Hau ab! +++ Lit = Literature +++

Mr Benn is a decent man, in the wrong job probably. He certainly thinks so today. When he walks into the classroom, it's clear: he knows what's gone on, as does Mrs Randall, our headmistress, who's with him. It must be serious.

Mrs Randall has on the same hat that she wore to my grandmother's funeral and she looks just as sad as she did that day. She doesn't waste time. She coughs and **adjusts** her hat. "Miss Bardwell deeply **regrets** her actions in the school grounds this morning. She has since offered her **resignation** to me and I have accepted it. Miss Bardwell felt that she had brought shame upon the school …"

WOOSHHSSHSS! It feels like a giant **hoover** has just **sucked** all the air out of the room. Mr Benn looks amazed. I don't think even he knew that part!

Mrs Randall nods briskly. She goes on and on: "Miss Shaw will **stand in** as your housemistress for the time being and Latin will be covered by …" but no one is listening. We won. The good guys actually won, do you **dig**? That never happens! It's incredible. Everyone is whispering excitedly. It feels like a **Mexican wave** might happen.

After Mrs Randall has **released** us, I break yet another rule and **scoot** upstairs to get my mobile, that's locked away. I have to call Nora, see how she is and tell her what's

+++ to adjust – zurechtrücken +++ to regret – bedauern +++ resignation – Kündigung +++ hoover – Staubsauger +++ to suck – saugen +++ to stand in – einspringen für +++ to dig – *hier:* kapieren +++ Mexican wave – La-Ola-Welle +++ to release s.b. – jmdn. entlassen +++ to scoot – rennen +++

happened. I switch it on. I hold my breath for a second … maybe Chris …

About 800 litres of blood rush to my face when I think of him. He doesn't have my mobile number to call me – he hardly knows me, I think, miserably. And yet I jumped on him today! Maybe he and Nora are both at the police station now, both reporting attacks. Nightmare.

I'm about to ring Nora when I notice that Maudie has called me twice. She's left a message on my mailbox and I listen to it. I haven't spoken to her in more than a week, not since we fell out about Matt. *Emily, the whole school is talking about what happened. You're a total legend. And I'm really sorry about the fight about Matt. You were right. He told me to give him some more space last week. We're still together but he's warned me. I'll tell you about it another time. Oh, before I forget, all of the girls thought that Jack Wolfskin was totally hot. I thought you said he was ugly? Sure you don't fancy him? Call me when you can.*

Wow. That's great that she's talking to me again and, well, good, I think, that she's still with Matt. Oh, I'll call her later. And I can't think about Jack Wolfskin.

I started this **surrounded** by Dark Things, remember? I needed Sam to protect me. Now, I don't feel like I need protecting any more. Maybe that was the important thing Grandma really had to tell me; *Emily, you can do it!*

And, even though that probably wasn't exactly what she wanted to say to me, I decide it definitely was. I can do it. Yes, that was *definitely it.*

+++ surrounded by – umringt von +++

Von Joanna Thompson in der Reihe "Freche Mädchen – Easy English!" ebenfalls erschienen:

Girls' School – *England Calling*
Girls' School – *The Ed Affair*
Girls' School – *Season of Love*
Girls' School – *Stand by your Sam*
Girls' School – *Long Distance Kisses*

Thompson, Joanna:
Girls' School – Vote for Love
ISBN 978 3 522 50136 1

Reihengestaltung und Gesamtausstattung: Birgit Schössow
Innentypografie: Kadja Gericke
Schrift: Minion und LTT Tapeside
Satz: KCS GmbH, Buchholz/Hamburg
Reproduktion: Medienfabrik, Stuttgart
Druck und Bindung: Friedrich Pustet, Regensburg

5 4 3 2 1° 10 11 12 13

www.planet-girl-verlag.de
www.frechemaedchen.de